EVERYMAN'S THEOLOGY

EVERYMAN'S THEOLOGY

Leo Von Rudloff, O.S.B.

Translated from the
Eighth German Edition

by

the Benedictine Fathers
of St. John's Abbey
Collegeville, Minnesota

THE BRUCE PUBLISHING COMPANY
MILWAUKEE

Imprimi potest: ALCUINUS DEUTSCH, O.S.B.
Nihil obstat: H. B. RIES, Censor librorum
Imprimatur: ✠ MOYSES E. KILEY, Archiepiscopus Milwaukiensis

March 4, 1942

Authorized translation from eighth German edition, published by arrangement with Verlag Friedrich Pustet, Regensburg, Germany. With the latest
(10th) edition, printed in Regensburg in 1940, the German text of this book
has reached a distribution of 30,000 copies in Germany and Switzerland.

(Third Printing — 1943)

AUTHOR'S PREFACE

IT IS a fortunate coincidence that this translation, begun
several years ago, appears after the author himself has come
to this country. He is happy to join the translators and the
publisher in presenting this little book to the American
public. During three years of teaching theology in the Immaculate Conception Seminary at Darlington, New Jersey,
he has had the privilege of getting in contact with the American mind. He has learned to love it sincerely.

It is an agreeable duty to acknowledge here the valuable
assistance of Dom Columban Quinn, O.S.B., in comparing
the translation with the original text. This book will appear
just when another enterprise which the author undertook
together with some confreres is getting on its way: the new
foundation whence these lines are written.

LEO RUDLOFF, O.S.B.

St. Paul's Priory, Keyport, N. J.

v

TRANSLATORS' PREFACE

IN A day when the forces of materialism have grown strong and powerful, it becomes more important than ever that we have a laity who has well-informed convictions in regard to the primacy of supernatural values. It will ever be true that "the just one lives by faith" (Heb. 10:38). In order that this faith be articulate and operative, however, it must needs be an intelligent faith. Religious instruction for the great majority of the laity was confined to the grade schools, supplemented by the Sunday sermon and some fragmentary reading. The object of presenting this volume to an English-reading public is to make available a complete treatise on all of the dogmatic truths of our religion — a treatise that gives a panoramic view of the "eternal liturgy" from when time had no beginning, unto the consummation of all things in the Godhead when faith will blend into vision.

In a single volume it was necessary to treat the various dogmatic truths succinctly; the approach to this book must therefore be one of prayer and meditation. The author has happily succeeded in integrating individual truths into that one all-embracing dogma of the mystical body, the very soul of which is the liturgy. If one of the objectives of the liturgy is to reproduce in our own person the life of Christ, then

EVERYMAN'S THEOLOGY can be recommended as a most practical guide.

And lest the title be misleading, the volume should have equal appeal and utility to clergy and laity alike. The possibilities of its use in discussion clubs are almost unlimited.

THE TRANSLATORS

Feast of All Saints, 1941

FOREWORD

THE title of this little book, EVERYMAN'S THEOLOGY, should arouse the interest of the intelligent Catholic who is desirous of having sound, concrete knowledge of his religion and of making that knowledge practical in his everyday life. Too often even so-called well-instructed Catholics are content with "believing" the truths of their holy religion without "knowing" them. As a consequence, to borrow a thought from St. Paul, they are not able to "give a reason for the faith that is in them." Knowing means more than merely believing. It implies something more personal and practical, more intimate and confidential than believing requires. Can the Catholic layman, then, pretend to, much less profess, a knowledge of the truths of faith (in all of which he believes), unless he studies those truths in themselves and in their relation to each other. Though he believes, his insufficient knowledge sometimes embarrasses him and keeps a sincere inquirer after the truth from embracing the true faith. Such a Catholic may try to quiet his conscience by telling his inquirer to go to the priest, which in almost every instance will not be done. It is not to the priest that the sincere but timid non-Catholic addresses the question that has been disturbing his soul, but to the Catholic man or woman alongside of him at the workbench or lunch counter, or in the bus or railroad train. Will the rather stupid suggestion: "Go to the priest" be taken in cases like this? And the reader knows that such cases are of daily occurrence. The obligation of the practical Catholic, then, both to himself and to his neighbor is clear.

EVERYMAN'S THEOLOGY is a very useful aid in the fulfillment of the serious obligation, incumbent upon all Catholics, of keeping themselves thoroughly instructed on the truths of faith, and of having a ready answer when their non-Catholic neighbor asks an intelligent question concerning those truths. The author is experienced in teaching theology to young aspirants to the priesthood who immediately after their ordination will labor in the parishes of several dioceses for the good of souls. In this little book he has adapted the same eternal and unchangeable truths to the needs of the layman in his everyday life. His teaching labors, therefore, should be doubly fruitful, carrying with them the authority and the confidence justified by his position as a learned professor of sacred theology.

May this little book fall into the hands of many Catholics who not only "believe" but wish to "know" more thoroughly the truths of their holy faith, and of many non-Catholics who are making a sincere and zealous effort "to come to a knowledge of the truth."

✠ WILLIAM A. GRIFFIN
Bishop of Trenton

Feast of All Saints, 1941

CONTENTS

PART I

GOD AND HIS ETERNAL PLAN OF CREATION AND SALVATION

PART II

EXECUTION OF THE PLAN OF REDEMPTION

PART III

APPLICATION OF THE REDEMPTION: OUR SANCTIFICATION

EVERYMAN'S THEOLOGY

CHAPTER I

THE CATHOLIC FAITH

1. RELIGION

RELIGION is the active realization of man's relation to God (cf. Appendix II A). Religion embraces the whole man with his intellect, will, and heart. It is a basic energy permeating, transforming, and shaping the whole life of man in all its phases, and referring all things and activities in that life to God as their last end. Religion is truth and life. It comprises, first, the knowledge of God and His relation to creatures and, second, the recognition of God by practical homage or worship[1] and by readiness to direct one's whole life toward God. Thus will union with God, which is man's destiny, be effected. These three elements stand in such intimate relation to one another that acknowledgment of their truth begets the rule for practical conduct. Man must clearly and definitely recognize the end and purpose of his existence before he can devote himself to their attainment. A well-defined aim is the first prerequisite for resolute and energetic

[1] For the present we are not concerned whether this worship is purely internal, or whether it must be given exterior expression. Suffice it to say that necessity for public worship derives not only from divine ordinance but also from the spiritual-corporeal and social nature of man. The community of mankind is likewise bound to render worship; but the purely interior acts of an individual do not have this social character.

action. Whence it follows that knowledge of the truth is always pregnant with vital values, and that practical life wells forth from the deep spring of truth. Religion is — as it will be explained later — not only the task of the individual but of the community as well.

A treatise on religion will, accordingly, consist of instruction, first, on the doctrines of faith, second, on moral conduct, and, third, on the worship of God. The object of the present work is to set forth the content of the deposit of faith which is in the possession of the Catholic Church. Moral theology and liturgy will not be developed as such; at most, their main doctrines will be indicated in so far as they are elements of true religion and have a necessary connection with the whole.

2. REVELATION AND FAITH

God alone through His merciful revelation and manifestation can show and make accessible the way which leads to Him.[2] This revelation was made in bygone times through men who spoke by the command and inspiration of God — whence they are styled prophets, or heralds of the divine Will.[3] This, however, was only preliminary. Revelation in the full sense of the term was made by *Jesus Christ*. The

---

[2] It should be noted that some truths of revelation can be attained by the use of reason alone, e.g., the immortality of the soul. Nevertheless, according to the Vatican Council, revelation of such truths is morally necessary so that "they may be known easily and certainly by all, without the admixture of error." The essential elements of Christian doctrine, however, are beyond the powers of human intelligence. Therefore, they must come to us through divine revelation, and must be believed because God has given testimony of them.

[3] According to Catholic teaching God made certain revelations to our first parents. Theologians hold that these proto-revelations also touched on the mysteries of the Trinity and the Incarnation. Through oral tradition these revelations were perpetuated in the literature of peoples — although at times with the admixture of much error.

activities of the prophets and patriarchs were preliminary and were intended to lead up to Christ. Christ, by His many miracles and above all by His Resurrection, gave incontestable proof that He had been sent by God to bring the truth to men. According to His own testimony, He was the Son of God made man, the Incarnate Truth: "I am the way, and the truth, and the life" (John 14:6). He is the manifestation of God and of eternal Truth in the flesh. He is *the* revelation of God, and to this revelation man responds by faith. The essential nature of faith is, therefore, the affirmation or the acceptance of Christ. As such, then, faith is a spiritual contact with Christ: "To have Christ dwelling through faith in your hearts" (Eph. 3:17). The Saviour likens faith in Himself, considered as a spiritual vision, to that vision of the brazen serpent in the desert which enabled the ancient Israelites to save themselves from bodily death (John 3:14–18). By virtue of this spiritual contact man draws eternal life for himself from Christ (John 5:24; 20:31; etc.). Hence "believing" is a vital, quickening contact with Christ, the Son of God and (since Christ is the Word of the Father) through Him, with the Father. Faith, as an essentially supernatural act, can come about only by God's grace, which makes the faculties of the human soul receptive of divine things. But at the same time, faith is a free and voluntary surrender of the entire man to Christ, the Incarnate Son of God. "Believing" means interior enrichment and also certainty regarding oneself and the purpose of one's being and life.

Since divine truth is obviously received by men in a human way, it has to be clad in such ideas and words as men can readily grasp. The significance of a "formula of faith," a dogma, a "definitely formulated truth of faith," and the necessity of guarding this formula in order that it may suitably express the Divine Truth, is evident. We must, of course, remember that no dogma can completely express the supernatural truth to be conveyed.

From the impulse arising out of love for divine truth springs the desire to assimilate more and more fully the content of a dogma. From it also arises the desire to systematize the truths of faith and to render them presentable for teaching. This in brief is the object of theology.[4]

Since nature and revelation have one and the same God for their author, there can be no contradiction between faith and reason. Seeming contradictions do occasionally occur; however, in such instances either something has been stated as a truth of faith, that is really *not* such, or, and this is more often the case, something is presented as a scientific conclusion that, after thorough investigation, is proven to be an error. Man is too easily inclined to draw unwarrantable conclusions from a given set of facts, e.g., from the admitted dependency of certain spiritual activities upon bodily conditions, he denies the freedom and spirituality of the soul, which can be deduced as a certainty from at least an equal number of observed facts.

3. THE TEACHING OFFICE OF THE CHURCH

Christ, we know, left this earth after His Resurrection and Ascension, entrusting to the Church the continuation of the work He had begun. He chose to leave behind Him not a dead, written letter, but a living authority (*magisterium*). The spoken word has always been for mankind the more vivifying and compelling force. The merely written word

[4] In the elaboration of articles of faith the Church permits a certain latitude for discussion. Thus we have different schools of theology which propose different ways of explanation, all approved or tolerated by the Church, but expressing the same deposit of faith.

can never entirely replace oral tradition and instruction. First of all, adapting Himself to this fact, Christ chose a group of men, the Apostles, to whom He assigned the task of teaching all mankind; they in turn appointed, as He had commanded, their successors, the bishops. Second, He bestowed a special pre-eminence upon one of the Apostles, St. Peter, whose successor by divine ordinance is the pope, the bishop of Rome.

On the day of His Resurrection Christ appeared to the Apostles gathered in the Cenacle and said to them: "Peace be to you! As the Father has sent me, I also send you." When He had said this, He breathed upon them, and said to them: "Receive the Holy Spirit; whose sins you shall forgive, they are forgiven them; and whose sins you shall retain, they are retained" (John 20:21–23). Here the Saviour gave the Apostles the command to teach and sanctify men that He had received from His heavenly Father. Shortly before His Ascension, He repeated the command in an especially solemn manner, when He appeared in the midst of His disciples and said to them: "All power in heaven and on earth has been given to me. Go, therefore, and make disciples of all nations, baptizing them in the name of the Father, and of the Son, and of the Holy Spirit, teaching them to observe all that I have commanded you; and behold, I am with you all days even unto the consummation of the world" (Matt. 28:18–20). With the Resurrection Christ inaugurated His rule of the whole world. In the consciousness of this power He now sent forth His disciples, confiding to them His own mission.[5] In the words of Christ: "He who hears you, hears me: and he who rejects you, rejects me" (Luke 10:16).

[5] Christ transmits to the disciples His threefold office of teacher, shepherd, and priest.

That his mission was to last for all time is evident from
the comforting assurance given by Christ to the disciples:
"Behold, I am with you all days even unto the consummation
of the world." To the end of time there will be souls to
whom God's word must be preached and to whom the sacraments must be administered. Therefore the Apostles had to,
and as an historical fact did, appoint successors. During the
time the Apostles were exercising supreme direction over the
communities which they had established, they appointed a
body of "Elders" (Greek: *presbyteroi* — whence the term
"priest" is derived), who were sometimes called "over-
seers," or bishops (Greek: *episcopoi*). Hence, originally the
designations "bishop" and "priest" were used interchange-
ably. When St. Paul journeyed to Jerusalem before his captivity, he disembarked at Miletus. As he found it impossible
to visit Ephesus, where a flourishing church had been founded by him, he sent there for the presbyters of the church and
addressed them, saying among other things: "Take heed to
yourselves and to the whole flock in which the Holy Spirit
has placed you as *bishops* [overseers], to rule the Church of
God" (Acts 20:17-28). Gradually the Apostles singled out
some individual "presbyter" and conferred special powers
upon him. Thus St. Paul sent as bishops Titus to rule the
church of Crete, and Timothy that of Ephesus: "For this
reason I admonish thee [Timothy] to stir up the grace of
God which is in thee by the laying on of my hands" (II Tim.
1:6). He also gives him instructions for his guidance: "Let
the presbyters who rule well be held worthy of double honor,
especially those who labor in the word and in teaching. . . .
Do not listen to an accusation against a presbyter unless it is
supported by two or three witnesses. When they sin rebuke
them in the presence of all that the rest also may have fear.

I charge thee before God and Christ Jesus and the elect angels, that thou observe these things impartially, in no way favoring either side. Do not lay hands hastily upon anyone and do not be a partner in other men's sins. Keep thyself chaste" (I Tim. 5:17–23). Timothy received his office of bishop by the imposition of Paul's hands. He in turn is to impose hands upon others over whom he has jurisdiction. "For this reason I left thee in Crete, that thou shouldst set right anything that is defective and shouldst appoint presbyters in every city, as I myself directed thee to do" (Tit. 1:5).

St. James the Younger (or Less), who is referred to in Holy Scripture as a "brother of the Lord" (Gal. 1:19), was the first bishop of Jerusalem.[6] As early as the time of St. Ignatius (d. 107 at Rome), martyr and bishop of Antioch, we find a hierarchy[7] of definite degrees. He writes to the congregation at Tralles that there can be no church without a bishop, presbyters, and deacons (Ep. to Trallians).[8] "All ye shall obey the bishop, as Jesus obeyed the Father; and also the priests as the Apostles; the deacons, however, as an ordinance of God" (Ep. to Smyrnaeans 8:1). "I stake my soul for those who are subject (or who submit) to the bishop, priests, and deacons" (Ep. to Polycarp 6:1). From this it is obvious that bishops are the legitimate successors of the Apostles, and that priests are the representatives and aids of the bishops. Thus we have an uninterrupted line of bishops from the time of the Apostles to the present day. This is what is meant by the "apostolic succession," whereby apostolical authority and doctrine have been handed down through the ages.

[6] Deacons are variously designated in the Epistles of St. Paul, e.g., Philippians 1:1; I Timothy 3:8–10, 12 f.

[7] In Greek hierarchy means holy government, body of holy officials.

[8] According to some theologians, subdiaconate and minor orders are later institutions of the Church; hence, they are not sacraments.

Upon His Apostle Peter, the Lord conferred a special office and mark of pre-eminence, that of the primacy. Christ had promised it at Caesarea Philippi. He had asked His disciples: " 'Who do men say the Son of Man is?' But they said: 'Some say John the Baptist; and others, Elias; and others, Jeremias, or one of the prophets.' He said to them: 'But who do you say that I am?' Simon Peter answered and said: 'Thou art the Christ, the Son of the living God.' Then Jesus answered and said: 'Blessed art thou, Simon Bar-Jona, for flesh and blood has not revealed this to thee, but my Father in heaven. And I say to thee, thou art Peter [Kepha, or rock], and upon this rock I will build my Church, and the gates of hell shall not prevail against it. And I will give thee the keys of the kingdom of heaven; and whatever thou shalt bind on earth shall be bound in heaven, and whatever thou shalt loose on earth shall be loosed in heaven' " (Matt. 16:13–20).

The primacy was promised to Peter under a threefold symbol: (1) he is to be the rock that ensures indestructible solidity to the Christian Church; (2) he is to be the master of the house, as the symbol of the keys suggests; (3) he is to receive the power of binding and loosing, that is to say, of remitting or retaining sins and of imposing or relieving from obligations; this last, conferred upon the Apostles as a body, is now conferred upon Peter personally. In Peter, therefore, are united the powers of all the Apostles.

In a special manner at the Last Supper, the Saviour once again promised Peter infallible firmness in faith and authority to teach: "Simon, Simon, behold Satan has desired to have *you* [pl.], that he may sift *you* [pl.] as wheat. But I have prayed for *thee,* that thy faith may not fail and do thou, when once thou hast turned again, strengthen thy brethren" (Luke 22:31, 32).

After the Resurrection Christ conferred the primacy upon St. Peter. Following the second miraculous draught of fishes on the Lake of Genesareth, Christ exacted of Peter, by way of reparation for his threefold denial of Him, a thrice repeated protestation of love: "Yes, Lord, thou knowest that I love Thee." And thrice the Lord replied: "Feed my lambs; feed my sheep" (John 21:15–17). Peter was thus appointed the shepherd and leader of the entire flock of Christ.

Soon afterward we find Peter exercising his primacy. He conducts the election of the Apostle Matthias and presides over the Council of the Apostles at Jerusalem. He delivers the first sermon on Pentecost and receives the pagan Cornelius into the Church. Paul, although he had been appointed an Apostle by Christ Himself, journeys to Jerusalem "to see Peter," and remains with him fifteen days (Gal. 1:18). When Peter declined to sit at table with converted Gentiles, his authority was considered so great that the attitude he assumed imperiled the future of the Gospel. For this Paul "withstood him to his face." Peter gave way and aligned his conduct with his own doctrinal decision (Gal. 2:12–14).

Since the Church is to exist for all time, even unto the consummation of the world, and because it is her task to continue Christ's mission everywhere and always, the primacy of Peter, the rock foundation of the Church, must be permanent. But who is Peter's successor in the primacy? It is a well-established fact that, from the very beginnings of Christianity, no church other than that of Rome ever claimed the primacy. The bishops of Rome always made that claim, basing it upon the fact that Peter died as Bishop of Rome, and that they are his successors in the Roman See.[9]

---

[9] The death and burial of St. Peter at Rome is now accepted as an unquestioned fact, although at one time is was bitterly contested by critics of the papacy.

In the eleventh century the Patriarchs of Constantinople attempted to usurp this primacy, asserting that New Rome (Constantinople) had replaced Old Rome. This is but one of many instances in which attempts were made to link the destiny of the Church with political institutions. The Roman pontiffs have successfully defended their right by pointing to the fact that Rome was adorned with the prerogative of the primacy not because she was the capital of the Empire[10] but because she was the see of St. Peter.

Evidences of the exercise of this primacy may be found in the earliest times. Even before the death of St. John the Apostle, Pope Clement in the year 96 writes an authoritative letter to the Church at Corinth, in Greece, where certain disorders were rife. In this letter we find the following significant passage: "If there be any who will not heed the words of Christ as spoken through us, let them know, that they are guilty of grievous sin and expose themselves to extreme peril" (59:1). In his letter to the Romans, St. Ignatius of Antioch, who was mentioned above, commends his diocese to the community at Rome which, he says with profound reverence, enjoys the pre-eminence in love ("love" here connotes "all the new elements that Christ's love brought into the world and that constitute the essence of Christianity" — *J. Thiele*). Although more proof can be given and many more authorities listed, we will conclude with the testimony of St. Irenaeus, bishop of Lyons, who died a martyr A.D. 202. He desires to set forth the true doctrine that was trans-

[10] It is not without significance, of course, that by a special arrangement of Providence the then capital city of the world was the center out of which radiated Christianity. Just as it was undoubtedly intended by the will of God that somewhat later the residence of the Caesars and with it the theater of political life should be moved to the East. Through these circumstances the papacy came into the exercise of her independent, spiritual influence over the world.

mitted from the Apostles down to his own time. For this purpose, he says, it would be advisable to trace in all Churches the succession of their bishops back to the Apostles themselves. As this, however, would be a very difficult task, he will confine himself to the Church of Rome. And that would suffice, for "every other Church must be in agreement with her (the Roman Church) by reason of her pre-eminence" (Adversus Haereses 3, 3, 2).

The pre-eminence of Peter and that of his successors, the bishops of Rome (the popes), comprise not only a primacy of honor (entitling him to the first place among all the bishops) but also a primacy of jurisdiction, namely, a direct, truly episcopal jurisdiction over the entire Church, commanding the obedience of *all* its members. It extends to whatever is required for the government of the Universal Church (Vatican Council).

4. INFALLIBILITY

The ecclesiastical teaching authority (*magisterium*) was instituted by Christ, in order that the Church might carry on even unto the end of time the mission received from Him by leading all men safely and surely to the knowledge of revealed truth and by preserving that truth undiminished and incorrupt. But this teaching body would be unreliable if it were subject to error or if men could not have the full assurance that it represented Christ, the Teacher of all truth; therefore, the ecclesiastical teaching authority must be endowed with *infallibility*. Christ Himself promised this to His disciples, and through them to the Church. At the Last Supper He promised it with: "Many things yet I have to say to you, but you cannot bear them now. But when he, the Spirit of truth, has come, he will teach you all truth" (John

16:12). The same is implied when He promises to be with
His disciples "all days even unto the consummation (or end)
of the world" (Matt. 28:20). For this reason St. Paul calls the
Church "the pillar and mainstay of truth" (I Tim. 3:15).
The promise of infallibility is unmistakable from the words
whereby the primacy is conferred upon Peter: he is to be
the rock foundation against which the gates of hell shall not
prevail; Christ prays for him that his faith will not fail but
will strengthen that of his brethren. This infallibility was
not granted to Peter alone but was to pass to his successors,
for it was to continue until the end of time. The passages
previously quoted from the early Fathers respecting the
primacy also bear witness to their faith in the infallibility
of the Church, and in particular of the Roman Church. The
Vatican Council, therefore, did not propose a new dogma
when it defined the infallibility of the pope.

Infallibility, however, was granted to the Church for a
very distinct purpose. Its limits are accordingly well defined,
in as much as it applies only to matters of *faith* and *morals*.
The Church is commissioned to propound faithfully the
teachings of Christ and to preserve them from all error
(Vatican Council); she was not endowed with infallibility
to decide purely natural questions. Because the Church is
required to interpret the teachings of Christ, the possibility
of progress and development in doctrines of faith suggests
itself. The body of revealed truth was indeed completed by
Christ[11] and there will never be an essentially new dogma or

[11] More correctly: with the death of the last Apostle. The Apostles were
chosen by Christ as the mediators of His revelation to mankind. Even Paul
(some years after the Resurrection of Christ) and John on the island of
Patmos (A.D. 96) received revelations that were directed to all mankind. All
later revelations made to individuals are "private" revelations and are binding on the recipient only.

article of faith. But the individual truths of revelation are not knowable and understandable to the same degree at all times. Thus with the progress of years a truth which has always been believed implicitly may become more clearly known and be proclaimed part of divine revelation by the teaching office of the Church. This is called "Development of Dogma" in the Catholic sense (cf. Appendix 4).

The teaching office of the Church is exercised in either the ordinary or extraordinary (solemn) form. The *ordinary* teaching authority expresses itself when a certain doctrine is proclaimed throughout the Church as being part of divine revelation. When the totality[12] of the bishops throughout the entire world propound a doctrine as having been revealed by God; or, when the faith of the Church in a doctrine becomes evident from universal custom or practice, from a formula of prayer universally used, and, above all, from the liturgy, such is a doctrine of faith. Anyone who refuses to embrace a universally accepted doctrine ceases to be a true believer. The Vatican Council and Pope Pius IX (1863) have explicitly acknowledged the teachings of the ordinary *magisterium* as true and authentic articles of faith. An instance of this ordinary teaching authority is the doctrine of the perpetual virginity of the Blessed Virgin Mary.

The *extraordinary* (solemn) teaching authority functions in one of two ways. First, General (Ecumenical) Councils assembled by the pope, who presides either in person or through legates and who must ratify the conclusions, define with infallible authority certain truths as doctrines of faith. Thus, the infallibility of the pope was defined by the Vatican Council. Second, the pope, in his capacity as Chief Teacher

---

[12] This "totality" is not disturbed if one or the other bishop deviates from the truth.

of Christendom officially (ex cathedra) proclaims a decision
or definition in matters of faith or morals, which then has
the force of law for the entire Church. Thus the dogma of
the Immaculate Conception of the Blessed Virgin Mary was
defined by Pope Pius IX in 1854. No Catholic attributes
either omniscience or *personal* (private) infallibility or even
impeccability to the pope or anyone. He does, however,
place his trust in the Holy Ghost abiding in the Church,
knowing that the Spirit of Truth will sustain Christ's representative on earth, when he, the pope, solemnly explains
articles of faith or morals contained in divine revelation.[13]
These extraordinary definitions are made as a rule only to
condemn heretical views or to counteract some other peril
to the faith. But to possess the fullness of Catholic doctrine
one must draw constantly from the living faith within the
Church; one must live with the entire Church, especially in
her liturgy, which is the expression of her fundamental
beliefs.

And so it is beyond dispute that *the immediate rule of
faith for man is the infallible teaching authority of the
Church*. Here man meets Christ Himself: "He who hears
you, hears me; and he who rejects you, rejects me" (Luke
10:16). No one can live in communion with Christ, unless
he submit to the authority of the Church; for by acknowl-
edging her authority to teach, he submits to Christ.[14]

[13] In exercising his office of supreme teacher, the pope is infallible only in
ex cathedra pronouncements. When he does not express his intention to
speak "ex cathedra," he is not infallible. The Roman congregations, who
assist the pope in the government of the universal Church, are not infallible. However, all decisions of the Holy See demand an interior religious
assent from the individual.

[14] One, who in good faith is not in visible communion with the Catholic
Church, can nevertheless have the good will to subject himself to her teaching
authority and thereby be in communion with Christ.

5. SOURCES OF FAITH

Christ has entrusted the entire body of revealed truth to the Church and she in turn transmits it to mankind through her infallible teaching. This revealed truth has been imparted in various ways. Some part of revelation was written down by the Apostles or their disciples under the direct inspiration of God; and this is the *Holy Scripture* of the New Testament. Another part of revelation has been transmitted orally; and this is *Tradition*.[15] Because the Church, especially in later centuries drew upon Holy Scripture and the Deposit of Tradition, e.g., the writings of the Fathers, in exercising her teaching authority, both Scripture and Tradition are considered sources of revelation or faith. In the order of time, Tradition precedes Scripture for the Christian faith already existed before there was a Holy Scripture of the New Testament, even as there was faith before the books of the Old Testament were written.[16] These sources are entrusted to the Church who safeguards, testifies to, and infallibly interprets them with the assistance of the Holy Spirit.

1. *Holy Scripture* is, as the Church teaches, "inspired," namely, written under the inspiration and guidance of the Holy Spirit. The Council of the Vatican teaches: "If anyone will not accept as sacred the books of Scripture whole and entire with all their parts, as enumerated by the Council of Trent, or will deny that they are divinely inspired: let him be anathema." The word "inspired" is indeed found in

[15] Likewise in the Old Testament, revelation was handed down by written and oral word.

[16] The first of the writings of the New Testament is St. Paul's first letter to the Thessalonians (cf. A.D. 51). By that time Paul had already done much of his missionary work, and Peter had preached and founded communities in Palestine. The first gospel — that of Matthew — was also written about this time.

Scripture, e.g., "All Scripture is inspired by God" (II Tim. 3:16). Pope Leo XIII, in his Encyclical "Providentissimus Deus" (Nov. 18, 1893), declared inspiration to be a positive divine influence upon the intellect, will, and faculties of the writer, whereby he wrote all and only those things which God Himself willed. It is not to be considered as a matter of verbal dictation nor as necessarily inseparable from revelation. We may best describe inspiration as did the early Fathers of the Church (Athenagoras, Gregory the Great) and later St. Thomas Aquinas (d. 1274) and Pope Leo XIII, by conceiving the relation between God and the human author as similar to that existing between a writer and his pen (St. Gregory the Great); or between a flute player and his flute (Athenagoras); or, speaking generally, between an agent and his instrument; or, in terms of philosophy, between a principal cause and an instrumental cause (St. Thomas and Leo XIII). Since Holy Scripture is the combined production of both God and man, we find in it characteristic evidences of the work of both.

Every book, every part of Holy Scripture (Vatican Council), every fact recorded, every thought expressed (Leo XIII), is inspired. As a consequence, Holy Scripture is absolutely free from error not only in matters of faith and morals but in all things, for God cannot teach error. It is necessary, of course, when interpreting the spoken or written word of an author, always to bear in mind what the author meant to impart. Scripture does not aim to instruct men concerning purely natural phenomena, historical, or scientific, but it is adapted to the mentality of those for whom it was written. Certainly, no one would accuse a preacher of error if, for the sake of example, he were to say: "When you, beloved Christians, contemplate the firmament by night and see the stars revolving about the earth . . ." He surely does not intend to explain the Ptolemaic or the Copernican system of planetary movement. Likewise, when reading the Bible, we must always bear in mind the purpose of the writer. We will thus, for instance, be able to distinguish poetic form and imagery (e.g., in the book of Job) from historical narrative.[17]

2. By Christian *Tradition,* as distinguished from Holy Scripture, we mean those revealed truths which Christ and the Apostles taught, but which were not at first written; they may have been recorded later on. Tradition is necessary for a twofold reason: first, that it may bear witness to *Scripture itself* (Tradition establishes what is Bible and what is not), and to the traditional interpretation of Scripture which has been handed down from generation to generation; second, tradition is also necessary *in addition* to Scripture as an independent and — as has been said above — an earlier source of revelation, since not all that Christ or the Apostles preached was written down. Thus, for example, definite proofs for the Immaculate Conception of the Blessed Virgin Mary could be derived only from Tradition, not from Scripture. In fact, Tradition is the living stream of faith flowing through the Church and embracing Holy Scripture itself.

6. FORMULAS OF FAITH: SYMBOLS OR CREEDS

To conclude this introductory chapter, we shall mention the more important Creeds in which, since the earliest days of Christianity, the chief articles of the Catholic faith have been contained.

---

[17] Only the original text is inspired, not the various translations. The so-called "Vulgate" edition of Holy Scripture is "authentic" in so far as dogmatic truths may be taken from it without error. However, the Church has never declared the "Vulgate" free from all textual error. She encourages all attempts to secure as accurate translations from the original as possible.

1. The Apostles' Creed, in its present form, probably dates from the fifth century. It was preceded by an older creed of almost identical content, which came into existence between A.D. 80–140, and which for its substance undoubtedly goes back to the time of the Apostles. Accordingly, this Creed, which is commonly recited with the Divine Office and the Rosary, has been appropriately called the Apostles' Creed. It begins: *Credo in Deum* — "I believe in God."

2. The Nicene-Constantinopolitan Creed was compiled during the General Councils of Nice (325) and Constantinople (381) to oppose the anti-Trinitarian heresies. This Creed is recited during Mass and begins: *Credo in unum Deum* — "I believe in one God."

3. The so-called Athanasian Creed, formerly ascribed to St. Athanasius (d. 373) but compiled somewhat later, perhaps in Spain, is still found in modern Breviaries. It begins with the words: *Quicumque vult salvus esse* — "Whoever wishes to be saved."

OUTLINE OF THE BOOK

The divine truths are not a group of unattached doctrines; they are rather the one divine life made accessible in Christ. Therefore the mystery of Christ, "the mystery which has been hidden for ages and generations, but now is clearly shown to his saints" (Col. 1:26), is at their center, giving unity and force to the whole. St. Paul was sent to proclaim this mystery, which he summarized in the words: *"Christ in you, your hope of glory"* (Col. 1:27). Christ, moreover, is the way to the Father, "I am the way" (John 14:6), and He achieves our sanctification through His Spirit, the Holy Spirit: "Because through him (Christ) we both have access in one Spirit to the Father" (Eph. 2:18).

St. Paul presents these central ideas in the first chapter of his Epistle to the Ephesians (1:3–14), where he chants a hymn to God and His work of Redemption (cf. Appendix II B):

God the Father chose us from all eternity to be His children in Christ.

God in the "fullness of time" sent His Son as the Redeemer who, with His blood, achieved the remission of man's sins and was made the focal point of the universe.

God the Holy Spirit was given us as a pledge of that eternal glory, of which we are heirs.

Therefore our treatise will be divided into three parts:

1. *God and His Eternal Plan of Creation and Salvation:* The triune God; Creation; Salvation.

2. *Execution of the Plan of Salvation:* Original Sin, Redemption; Christ's Sacrifice on the Cross and His Resurrection.

3. *Application of the Redemption:* Christ and the Holy Ghost; the Church, the Body of Christ; the sacraments; the consummation in eternity.

This division is also to be discerned throughout the ecclesiastical year (cf. Appendix II C).

PART I

GOD AND HIS ETERNAL PLAN OF CREATION AND SALVATION

CHAPTER II

THE TRIUNE GOD

1. THE MOST HOLY TRINITY

ST. PAUL'S hymn of praise in the first chapter of the Epistle
to the Ephesians begins with the words: "Blessed be the God
and Father of our Lord Jesus Christ." From God the Father
all good comes and to Him all good returns. "Every good
gift and every perfect gift is from above, coming down from
the Father of lights" (James 1:17). The mystical fact that
God is a Father and has a Son suggests the mystery of the
Most Holy Trinity, of which we shall now speak. This mystery will become vital to us when we realize its importance
in God's redemptive work. The objective of this book is to
show the connection between the mysteries of the Most Holy
Trinity and the Redemption as we have indicated above.
The following remarks, therefore, must be understood in
relation to the later chapters which treat of the Redemption.

Christ calls God His Father but He never speaks of Him
as "our Father." God is not His Father in the same sense that
He is the Father of the disciples for He is "My Father and
your Father." Christ is the Son of God in a special sense and
He alone can say of His Father: "I and the Father are one"
(John 10:30). Christ also speaks frequently of the Holy
Spirit who proceeds from the Father and who will be sent

by Christ Himself or by the Father in Christ's name, to act as Sanctifier, Paraclete, and Advocate in Christ's stead and as the teacher of divine truth in all its fullness. The Trinity revealed Itself at the baptism of Christ in the Jordan: The Son made man was baptized, the Father's voice came from heaven, and the Holy Spirit descended upon Christ in the form of a dove. Our Lord expressed the mystery of the Holy Trinity to the disciples shortly before His Ascension: "All power in heaven and on earth has been given to me. Go, therefore, and make disciples of all nations, baptizing them in the name of the Father, and of the Son, and of the Holy Spirit" (Matt. 28:18–19). He who believes is to receive re-mission of sin and justification by baptism in the *one name* of the Father, and of the Son, and of the Holy Ghost. In the letters of the Apostles frequent mention of the Blessed Trinity is made. Thus St. Paul concludes his second letter to the Corinthians with these words: "The grace of our Lord Jesus Christ, and the charity of God [the Father] and the fellowship of the Holy Spirit be with you all" (II Cor. 13:13). In his letter to the Ephesians the Apostle says: "Because through him [Christ] we both have access in one Spirit to the Father" (Eph. 2:18).

Faith in the Holy Trinity is as living today as it was in the past. We have it, for instance, in the rite of baptism: "In the name of the Father, and of the Son, and of the Holy Ghost." Again, in the Apostles' Creed and in the so-called doxologies: "Glory be to the Father and to the Son and to the Holy Ghost." Finally it is found in the conclusions of liturgical prayers (collects, orations), e.g., "Through our Lord Jesus Christ who liveth and reigneth with Thee in the unity of the Holy Spirit, God forever and ever. Amen."

There is then one God in three Persons, and by name

these three Persons are the Father, the Son, and the Holy Spirit. These names express the relationship existing between the three Persons, a relationship based upon origin. Theologians speak of "processions" in God, and the relations based upon these "processions" make it possible to distinguish these Persons one from another. In all else they are perfectly identical for they possess *one* common essence and are *one* God, mutually compenetrating one another. This doctrine is set forth by the Council of Florence (1438–45) in the following terms: "The Holy Roman Church professes . . . one true, almighty, immutable God, the Father, the Son, and the Holy Spirit, one in essence, triune in person: the unbegotten Father, the Son begotten by the Father, and the Holy Spirit proceeding from the Father and from the Son. The Father is neither the Son nor the Holy Spirit; the Son is neither the Father nor the Holy Spirit; the Holy Spirit is neither the Father nor the Son; but the Father is only the Father; the Son is only the Son; and the Holy Spirit is only the Holy Spirit. God the Father alone begot the Son out of His own [the Father's] substance; the Son alone is begotten by the Father alone. The Holy Spirit alone proceeds from the Father and from the Son. These three Persons are one God and not three Gods; for they all have one and the same substance, one essence, one nature, one divinity [or godhead], one immensity, one eternity. *All is one in God, save where an opposition of relationships exists.* In consequence of this unity the Father is wholly in the Son and wholly in the Holy Spirit; the Son is wholly in the Father and wholly in the Holy Spirit; and the Holy Spirit is wholly in the Father and wholly in the Son. None precedes the others in eternity [they are coeternal], nor exceeds them in majesty, nor excels them in power. From eternity and without a beginning, 'the Son has His being from the Father; from eternity and without a beginning, the Holy Spirit proceeds from the Father and from the Son. What the Father is or has, He has not received from another but of Himself; He is beginning without a beginning [source without a source]. What the Son is or has, He has from the Father: He is source from a source. What the Holy Spirit is or has, He has at the same time from the Father and from the Son. But the Father and the Son are not two principles of the Holy Spirit, but only one principle; even as the Father, the Son, and the Holy Spirit are not three principles [causes] of creation but only *one* principle." This is an inscrutable mystery of faith for no finite and human intellect would ever have discovered a trinity of Persons in one God.[1]

Although the mystery of the Holy Trinity surpasses human understanding, it is not contrary to reason. We do not say that three is equal to one, or three natures are one nature, or three Persons are one Person; but that three Persons are one nature. The eagerness of the mind to fathom this mystery moved the Fathers of the Church to render it more accessible by the use of images and similitudes or analogies.[2] In order to illustrate the relationship between the Father, Son, and Holy Spirit, they pointed to natural trinities like the sun, its rays, and its light; or a spring, stream, and river. Gradually they began to use analogies found in the mental life of man: mind, thought, and will. A prolific source for such similitudes is the passage in Genesis (1:26) where God speaks of making man to His own

[1] Traces of the original revelations in regard to the Trinity have persisted among many nations and eminent thinkers (e.g., Plato).

[2] One of the more important tasks of theology is to facilitate the understanding of mysteries of faith by the use of proper analogies and examples that appeal to our mental faculties.

image and likeness. Another is the prologue to the Gospel of St. John in which the Second Person, the Son of God, is styled the "word" (*logos*). Before we speak a word, we must first have a clear idea in our mind. Before we say "man," we must first know what "man" means, i.e., we must have a concept of "man." This concept may be called our mental word, which precedes the spoken word. Now God has a complete, clear concept of Himself; He knows Himself; from all eternity He forms a perfect concept (idea) of Himself, and expresses His own being in the mental "word" that was in the beginning, was with God, and was God Himself (John 1:1). The concepts we form are poor, imperfect, lifeless; but God's word is the sum total of His own most perfect being; it is God Himself, the Son of God; it is the wisdom of God personified.[3]

It is much more difficult to find a similar analogy for the origin of the Third Person, the Holy Spirit. But here too, we can fall back upon our mental processes, and from them establish an analogy with love or will. Father and Son love one another with a love so real that it constitutes the Third Person. The Holy Spirit, as the Credo in the Mass has it, proceeds equally from the Father and from the Son. He is, so to speak, the bond of love, and therefore of unity, between Father and Son as distinct persons. He is likewise the expression of their love; and since love is the primary force and aggregate of all good dispositions, He is the expression of God's holiness. He is the spirit of holiness, the Holy Spirit.

This leads us to consider the practical value of the dogma of the Trinity in Christian life. The Holy Trinity is our goal; and participation in the triune life of God is the end

[3] In the Old Testament this truth became progressively clearer in the books of Wisdom and Ecclesiasticus.

for which, with the help of God's grace, we are striving. We cannot grasp the meaning of our life of grace if we have no knowledge of the Holy Trinity, for it is both the source and the goal of our supernatural life. The Trinity is also the exemplar of our social life, for in it we find the most perfect adjustment between self-assertion on the part of the individual and devotion to the common welfare. With human beings personal and social tendencies too often lead only to conflict; but in God all such conflict is excluded. Consequently, we can achieve victory over such conflicts within ourselves only by participating in God and by our increased growth in the triune God. This will result from a continued development of the life of grace within us. The doctrine of the Holy Trinity is, therefore, the dogma of the *living* God. In Him life finds expression in mutual possession, in mutual surrender, in mutual intercommunion. God is the life of which all other life is but a shadowy image.

2. GOD THE FATHER: NATURE AND ATTRIBUTES OF GOD

The Father is the source and the sum total of the divine essence which He shares with His consubstantial Son. From the Father and from the Son this self-communication of the divine nature overflows to the Holy Spirit. For this reason the theologians predicate of the Father, in whom the divine nature is found as in its source and origin, everything concerning that nature.

The Council of the Vatican (Session III) briefly and compactly states the Catholic doctrine regarding God as follows: "The holy, catholic, apostolic, and Roman Church believes and professes one true and living God, Creator and Lord of heaven and earth, almighty, eternal, immense, incomprehensible, infinite in intellect and will and in every kind of perfection. Since He is a single, entirely simple, and immutable spiritual substance, it must also be acknowledged that He is really and of His very nature distinct from the world; in Himself and of Himself perfectly happy and indescribably far above everything that is outside of Himself or that can be thought of." This is the Catholic faith concerning God as it comes down to us from the preaching and teaching of Christ, in whom the revelation of the Old Testament was fulfilled.

Before undertaking a detailed exposition of these doctrines, we must keep in mind that the Council of the Vatican teaches that God is "incomprehensible and indescribably far above everything that is outside of Himself or that can be thought of." In all that we say about God we must always remain conscious of the fact that our knowledge of Him is inadequate. We do not know God as He really is in Himself — in the way we shall see Him in eternity; we can acquire only a faint knowledge of Him by contemplating His works. St. Thomas Aquinas tells us that we do not so much know what God *is,* as what He is *not.* According to St. Thomas we can derive some knowledge of God from the imperfection of creatures through *affirmation, comparison,* and *negation,* i.e., we affirm of God all perfection to be found in creatures; then we extend these perfections at once to an infinite degree; and, finally, we eliminate from Him all imperfections, defects, limitations, and bounds discernible in created beings. Thus we arrive at a realization of these two truths: (1) that God is entirely "different" from all creatures; and (2) that all creatures are but images or semblances of the Creator.

1. *The Essence of God:* God is a spirit, i.e., an incorporeal, immaterial being endowed with intellect and free

will who is not perceptible by our senses but is comprehensible only by our intellects. The opinion that a spirit is a tenuous, refined body is definitely and totally false. A spirit may more correctly be compared to a thought which has real existence even though we cannot see it; or to the ideas of justice, truth, and the like which are real, even though we cannot grasp or touch them.

God is a being that thinks itself, i.e., a being that is at once the "thinker" and the "thought." His own essence in which He knows all created things is the first and proper object of His knowledge. An act of "knowing" is followed by one of "willing," which in turn expresses itself either in "affirming" (loving) or "denying." God wills, i.e., loves Himself; He also wills, or loves, all creatures, in so far as they are in accord with His being. He must then hate all that is at variance with His being, all that is destructive to the divine in the creature, i.e., sin.

The most profound concept of His being was revealed by God Himself to Moses in the burning bush. When God was about to send him to lead the Israelites out of Egypt, Moses asked the Lord: "If they should say to me: What is his name? What shall I say to them? God said to Moses: I am who am [I am the I-am]. Thus shalt thou say to the children of Israel: He who *is,* hath sent me to you" (Exod. 3:13–14). The nature of God has never been described more perfectly. Being of itself (*a se*); being without change or addition — such is the essence of God. And this being is at the same time an act of intellection and of will. God is, therefore, a person, a personal being, and not an indefinite, vague, impersonal entity or principle. Since He is a pure, perfect Spirit, God is *"simple,"* i.e., not composite, not consisting of parts. All is one in Him. He is distinct and different from the composite imperfect world which He governs as Creator and free Ruler.

From this idea of God as unlimited, unqualified "being," it follows that He possesses all attributes without limitation, i.e., He is infinitely perfect. Whatever good we can think of is in God to an infinite degree: since He is the fullness of goodness, of all perfection, God is "*one*." There can be but one "all-goodness," one being without limitation and possessing every perfection, otherwise it would not be infinite.

2. *The Divine Attributes:* Although being, knowing, and willing are one in God, we must consider them as separate. So we speak, necessarily, of the attributes of God's being or essence, of His divine intellect, and of His divine will.

a) Attributes of God's Essence. First, God is *eternal* and *immutable.* The two concepts must be associated, for "eternity" means being without beginning or end, and also, being without succession or change of any kind. To God there is no yesterday and no tomorrow, only an eternal "now." "Before the mountains were made, or the earth and the world was formed, from eternity and to eternity thou *art* God" (Ps. 89:2). (Note the present tense of the verb.)

Second, God is *omnipresent* and *immense* (boundless). He is beyond space and beyond time; He is neither in space nor in time. His immensity is not that of a body without bounds or measurability for He is not an extended substance. When He creates a corporeal, material being, He is present to it as its cause or maker; and hence there can be no space, no body, to which God is not present. God's omnipresence follows from His omnipotence, in virtue of which He governs and controls every created cause. "Whither shall I go from thy spirit? or whither shall I flee from thy face? If I ascend into heaven, thou art there: if I descend into hell, thou art present. If I take my wings early in the morning, and dwell in the uttermost parts of the sea: even there also shall thy hand lead me; and thy right hand shall hold me" (Ps. 138:7–10).

b) *Attributes of God's Knowledge:* First, God is all knowing or *omniscient;* He knows the past, the present, and the future, even our most hidden thoughts. Unlike us, God does not draw His knowledge from things, in such a manner that these things cause His knowledge of them, but rather His knowledge precedes things and causes them. God does not know things because they are, but they are such because God knows them.

Second, God is *all wise.* Over and above God's omniscience, His infinite wisdom implies planning, foresight, and ordering in the divine control of the world and history. Moreover it includes His providence, to which all things, great and small, are subject: "Oh, the depth of the riches of the wisdom and of the knowledge of God! How incomprehensible are his judgments and how unsearchable his ways! For 'Who has known the mind of the Lord, or who has been his counsellor? Or who has first given to him, that recompense should be made of him?' " (Rom. 11:33–34.)

c) *Attributes of the Divine Will:* God is *almighty* because of the infinite power of His divine will. He can do all that He wills to do.[4] All that is not God Himself, was made by Him. Since God's will is identical with His essence, it is essentially united with the most perfect Being, with the supreme Good. From this follows God's *sanctity.* God cannot will anything but good, the sovereign good, which is Himself. To us the sanctity of God appears as something tre-

---

[4] Naturally, God cannot will anything that is contradictory in itself, e.g., a square circle, since that would contradict His own Being, in whom all things have their source.

mendous, and the vast difference between ourselves and the all-holy God is almost overwhelming and terrifying. Yet the thought of His holiness has for us something exceedingly consoling and positively uplifting, for His holiness is the source of our holiness. God's holiness does not tower above us like a threatening, unattainable, snow-covered summit; but it dispenses blessings and offers itself to us as a gift, thus enabling us to perfect the image of essential holiness in ourselves. It draws us up to Him, while imparting itself to us.

This emanation of divine perfection in all creatures is called God's *goodness*. "Goodness communicates itself" (*Bonum est sui diffusivum*) was a maxim of the old theologians. God shares His perfections with all creatures. "Every good gift and every perfect gift is from above, coming down from the Father of lights" (James 1:17). Since God wills the perfection of creation, He requires holiness and goodness from free creatures. He would have them all be perfect: "You therefore are to be perfect, even as your heavenly Father is perfect" (Matt. 5:48). According as the creature complies with this command, He will grant or refuse His gifts for God is *just*. But knowing the weakness and inadequacy of the creature, God is also *merciful*. He is always ready to make up for the weakness of the creature, if the latter admits it, by willingly forgiving the sinner who is contrite and disposed to mend his ways. And since God is *long-suffering* (patient), He refrains from punishing in order to give time for repentance. God's goodness and mercy are most splendidly revealed in Christ: "For God so loved the world that he gave his only begotten Son, that those who believe in him may not perish, but may have life everlasting" (John 3:16). In Christ we behold God's attributes embodied in human form.

From the perfection of God's will, in union with the perfection of His knowledge, result two additional divine attributes. First, God's *veracity* (truthfulness), i.e., God cannot
err, for His knowledge is identical with eternal Truth and
with perfect Being; nor can He lie, for His knowledge is one
with infinite sanctity. Second, God's *fidelity:* God will always
be true to His promises. Our staunch, unshaken faith is based
upon God's veracity, our firm hope is based upon His
fidelity.

For a correct knowledge of God's attributes, we must bear
in mind that since in God there is neither composition nor
division, one attribute must not be separated from another,
but each must be regarded as one with all the others. With
God and in God everything is one; He is the simplest of all
beings. But we must distinguish and consider now this, now
that aspect of His being, and designate His various attributes
by specific names because of our limited intellect. Actually,
for example, God's power or omnipotence is united, or rather,
identical with His justice, wisdom, and holiness. Likewise
God's justice is at the same time love, and His love, justice.
Consequently the divine attributes are not limited by the
bounds set for human virtues. Human virtues may conflict
one with another; our love for justice may, for instance, not
harmonize with our goodness. This is possible only because
our justice and our goodness are imperfect. "Justice without
mercy is cruelty; mercy without justice is the mother of
anarchy" (St. Thomas Aquinas). It is only when we mentally
remove all bounds or limitations that the attributes in God
become divine, i.e., infinitely perfect. Let us, therefore, here
again be reminded of the incompleteness of our knowledge
of God.

CHAPTER III

THE ECONOMY OF CREATION
AND REDEMPTION

1. THE ECONOMY OF CREATION

JESUS CHRIST, the second Person of the Blessed Trinity and the Word of God, is the *compendium* of divine wisdom, of divine knowledge. In Him God sees from all eternity His own substance and gives spiritual expression to it. But God also sees in this Word the many possibilities of expressing Himself still further, through created beings which will be images and reflections of the Word. Thus, the Son of God is also the spiritual compendium of all creation. Everything that God produces or will at any time produce, existed as thought from all eternity in the Word of God. Every human being has been in the mind of God as such a divine thought from all eternity. There is nothing in heaven or on earth that did not originate in God's wisdom. All that happens or ever will happen begins there.

There is therefore a divine thought concealed in every being and in every event; to search for and discover it is the privilege of the human mind. This divine thought, which is revealed in the creature's outward form and in states of being and activities, constitutes its very essence.

Upon this fact is founded our faith in Providence, in which we trust in every condition of life, and which gives us hope and peace of mind in all situations and circumstances. Christ speaks of it in these words: "Therefore I say to you do not be anxious for your life, what you shall eat; nor yet for your body, what you shall put on. Is not the life a greater thing than food and the body than the clothing? Look at the birds of the air: they do not sow or reap, or gather into barns; yet your heavenly Father feeds them. Are not you of much more value than they? But which of you, by being anxious about it, can add to his stature a single cubit? And as for clothing, why are you anxious? See how the lilies of the field grow; they neither toil nor spin, yet I say to you that not even Solomon in all his glory was arrayed like one of these. But if God so clothes the grass of the field which today is alive and tomorrow is thrown into the oven, how much more you, O you of little faith? Therefore do not be anxious, saying, 'What shall we eat?' or 'What shall we drink?' or 'What are we to put on?' (for after all these things the Gentiles seek); for your Father knows that you need all these things. But seek first the kingdom of God and his justice, and all these things shall be given you besides. Therefore do not be anxious about tomorrow; for tomorrow will have anxieties of its own. Sufficient for the day is its own trouble" (Matt. 6:25–34).

From among the countless possibilities of images or reflections of Himself, as contemplated by the eye of God, He selected only a few and willed them to *be*. This act of the divine will comprises the act of creation. What God wills, *is*. The things that God wills are *such* and *where* and *when* and *as long as* He wills them to exist.[1] But since "willing" is

---

[1] Just as the world was created by God, so it is also "sustained" by Him. God's providence in regard to the world is like a continued creation: He keeps all things in existence. Should He withdraw His sustaining hand, creation would again vanish into the nothingness from whence it sprang.

equivalent to "loving" (affirming), all creatures issue from the goodness and love of God as well as from His wisdom. Every creature owes its being to wisdom and love and therefore every creature bears in itself a vestige of the Holy Trinity.

A difficulty, however, might arise from the fact of suffering and evil. So far as suffering is concerned, a theoretical solution is comparatively easy, which may also serve as a practical motive for overcoming it.[2] Even suffering has a meaning and purpose for it has its source not in blind fate but in the wisdom and goodness of God. It exists, therefore, not for its own sake, but as a means toward the attainment of happiness. It is, indeed, often difficult for men to recognize this significance of suffering, for we cannot look into the designs of God, but strong faith will enable us to submit to the will of the Almighty. Furthermore we must remember that suffering is a consequence of *original sin*.

The existence of evil will be more fully discussed in the next chapter. Suffice it to say for the present that God does not in truth *will* evil, but only *permits* it. The source of evil is in the free will of man. A created being endowed with free will has liberty of action and therefore can abuse or misuse his freedom. Nevertheless it must be admitted that even evil somehow serves the designs of God and must place itself in the service of the wisdom and goodness of God. We cannot defeat the purposes of an omnipotent and omniscient Creator. He will eventually triumph!

[2] Undoubtedly the strongest motive is the thought of victory over suffering through Christ. Christ has made suffering a highway to salvation, so "that the sufferings of the present time are not worthy to be compared with the glory to come that will be revealed in us" (Rom. 8:18). As Christ went to His glory through suffering, so also shall we, if we become like unto Him in suffering.

Besides the visible world God has also designed and created an *invisible* one, i.e., the *Angels*. Holy Scripture speaks of them frequently. Thus, St. Paul writes: "For in Him were created all things in the heavens and on the earth, things visible and things invisible, whether Thrones, or Dominations, or Principalities, or Powers" (Col. 1:16). These last words imply that there are certain gradations ("choirs") among the angels, regarding which we know nothing more.[3] An angel is a pure bodiless spirit imperceptible to the senses. But it is endowed with intellect and free will, and is therefore a person. Theology teaches that all the angels were from the beginning endowed by God with sanctifying grace, but that a number of them sinned.[4] In the epistle of St. Jude (1:6) we read: "And the angels also who did not preserve their original state, but forsook their abode, he has kept in everlasting chains under darkness for the judgment of the great day." The sin of the angels could only have been pride, since a pure spirit can commit no other sin: pride is *the* sin of the spirit. Theologians unanimously hold that this sin was rebellion against God.

God employs the good angels in the government of the world. St. Thomas Aquinas expresses a beautiful thought when he writes that the entire visible world is under the protection of these pure and holy spirits. The stars are guided by them in their orbits, and the peoples of the earth

[3] Since the fourth century, theologians are accustomed to enumerate nine choirs of angels.

[4] The sin of the angels was evidently completed in a moment of time. St. Thomas holds as "more probable and more in consonance with the dicta of the saints" that the devil sinned immediately after his creation. A spirit of such perfection comprehends the extent and results of its decision in a moment. Hence there can be no repentance for the fallen angels. Man can alter his judgment with a change of circumstances, owing to his spiritual-corporeal make-up.

are entrusted to the keeping of these heavenly princes. In particular, every human being has a Guardian Angel.[5] In the liturgy we join the angels in chanting the Trisagion, the "thrice holy"; they carry our gifts to the heavenly altar in the sight of God. They will lead us into the realm of bliss, *In paradisum deducant te Angeli;* in fact, we are already there: "But you have come to Mount Sion, and to the city of the living God, the heavenly Jerusalem, and to the company of many thousands of angels" (Heb. 12:22).

The fallen angels or devils wage war with all the means at their command against the supernatural order. "They are the great disturbers of God's order" (Abbot Anscar Vonier, O.S.B.). Their power was great before the coming of Christ but, since His arrival, it has been checked: "Now will the prince of the world be cast out" (John 12:31). Their influence grows in the measure that men withdraw from Christ's influence. St. Augustine compares the devil to a chained dog, that can harm only those who recklessly go too near him. Therefore the Apostle says: "Do not give place to the devil" (Eph. 4:27). In the prayers after Mass the Church prays that St. Michael, the prince of the heavenly host, may "cast into hell Satan and the other evil spirits who roam about the world seeking the destruction of souls." The fearful reality of this wicked power cannot be denied in view of the widespread hatred of Christ that flares up everywhere. But "the prince of this world has already been judged" (John 16:11); Christ will win the final decisive victory.

The crown of visible creation is *man,* for whom God created the world; he is its lord and master. Holy Scripture

[5] According to strict interpretation, it is only a matter of faith that the angels watch over the human race as such, and that children have their guardian angels (Matt. 18:10). That each individual human being has a particular guardian angel is, however, a universal belief of long standing.

says of man that he was created an "image" of God. Although in a certain sense every being is an image of God, man in a special manner has been created according to the divine pattern. This likeness consists in man's natural spiritual faculties, in his intellect and will; he is the "natural image of God." When man came from the hand of God, all these faculties were still unclouded (normal) and gave man a truly royal dignity. By means of his spiritual endowments man was to discover the image of God in all things, and, by praise of their creator, he was to refer them to their source; in the words of Eckhart, the mystic: "Every creature strives to penetrate into man and his reason in order thereby to be brought back to God." In man, therefore, all creatures attain their significance. Man occupies, as it were, a priestly, i.e., a mediatorial position in the created world. He joins the world of matter with that of spirit and with God. With truth then early writers describe man as a *microcosm*, a world in miniature, but first and primarily he is the "supernatural image" of God.

Why did God create the world? It was not because of any need, necessity, or coercion, for God, the Triune, possesses in Himself infinite life and bliss. He created the world out of His abundant goodness and unto His own glory. Even though God possesses in the bosom of His triune life the superabundance of glory and honor, He desired to create beings who would participate in this glory. They shall give Him glory and in so doing realize their destiny, the gaining of eternal bliss.

2. THE ECONOMY OF SALVATION

According to the designs of the Almighty, nature was not created for its own sake. Since God created rational beings like unto Himself, he desired to enter into such intimate communion with them that they would participate in His own life. By an act of grace He desired to extend to the creature, as it were, the sonship by which the Second Person of the Holy Trinity is related to the heavenly Father. What is peculiar to the eternal Son by nature and is His substantially from all eternity, was to be communicated to the creature by participation through grace. In this way the creature would be drawn into the inner life of the Holy Trinity.

The privilege of participation in that sonship far exceeds all the rights and merits of a created nature. It is a supernatural gift and by it the creature is to attain to "super-creatural," divine perfection. Yet this supernatural perfection is quite in accord with what the created spirit is required to strive for to become perfect; for only in God may its yearnings be fulfilled and its faculties fully developed. "The supernatural realization of being, to which the theological virtue of hope tends, lies concealed under every natural hope. All our natural hopes aspire to fulfillment; they are like vague reflections and foreshadowings (adumbrations), like unconscious anticipations of life everlasting" (Joseph Pieper). Nature without supernatural perfection will ever remain a thing incomplete.[6] Supernature always perfects nature and never destroys it. Consequently, through the supernatural elevation of the creature, the end of created being — God's glory — is realized much more perfectly. Only the child of God can give the glory due to God. Nature of itself cannot conflict with grace; only *fallen* nature can do so. Or, in other words, created nature by conflicting

[6] God could have left the human creature in an incomplete and limited state. Only through an act of purest grace did he destine it to a supernatural perfection. The possibility of a state of pure nature was defended by the Church in 1567 against the errors of Michael du Bay (Baius) of Louvain.

with supernature "falls" and offends the Creator, as well as itself — as was exemplified in the sin of the angels.

The creature was elevated to *adoptive sonship* of God. This is evident from the fact that God embraces it with a father's love and extends to it the love which He bears His only-begotten Son. Since the manifestation of love within the Trinity is the Holy Spirit, we may say that God imparts His Spirit to the creature. He gives it the Holy Ghost. The latter transforms the creature into His own image and stamps upon it His own likeness, that is "sanctifying grace," a participation in God's nature, a deification. God "has granted us the very great and precious promises, so that through them you may become partakers of the divine nature" (II Pet. 1:4). This sanctifying grace manifests itself chiefly in a new, childlike love for the heavenly Father, with whom the creature has entered into such an intimate relationship. The Holy Spirit is the bond of union between the heavenly Father and the creature elevated to the dignity of an adopted child of God, as He is also the bond between the Father and the Son in the Holy Trinity.

Such was the original plan of God. But St. Paul writes, in the first chapter of his Epistle to the Ephesians, which serves as the basis of this work, that "He (God) predestined us to be adopted through Jesus Christ as his sons, according to the purpose of his will, unto the praise of the glory of his grace, with which he has favored us in his beloved Son" (Eph. 1:5–6). The Incarnation of the Son of God was, therefore, included in the eternal purpose of God to sanctify mankind. In order to appreciate this, we must keep the following in mind.

At the creation of man God had given the Holy Spirit as a dowry to the entire race in the person of the first man. A purely human progenitor, however, could forfeit the Holy Spirit for himself and his progeny, and actually did so. God foresaw the sin of Adam, but in order that mankind as such should never again be separated from the Holy Spirit, God chose to bestow Him in a manner designed from all eternity: God would Himself become man. Thus divinity and humanity would be forever inseparably bound together. St. Cyril of Alexandria (d. 444) says in his commentary on the Gospel of St. John (7:39): "God the Word, who is not subject to any change, became man, in order that He might preserve as man the gift (the Holy Spirit) for human nature forever more" (Bk. 5, Chap. 2).

Hence the Incarnation of the Son of God had been included in the design of God from the beginning. Through the God-Man, and through Him alone, did God unite Himself inseparably with human nature. It is no longer possible for the human race as such to be lost; the individual man can forfeit salvation but he can always regain it in the God-Man. Were it not for the Incarnate Word of God, this possibility could not exist. Moreover, the abundance of grace has been increased by the fact that the Son of God Himself chose to become a member of the human race. Thus each member of the race also has the power of greater perseverance and fidelity. But more about this later.

PART II

EXECUTION OF THE PLAN OF REDEMPTION

CHAPTER IV

NECESSITY OF REDEMPTION: ORIGINAL SIN

1. ORIGINAL JUSTICE

GOD executed His eternal plan of salvation in the beginning
of time. Man, male and female, came forth from the hands
of God splendidly endowed, with natural gifts of soul and
body intact. In addition he possessed sanctifying grace, which
made him a child of God and partaker of the nature of his
heavenly Father. Thus was man an "adopted" son of God,
not only juridically (in a legal sense) but also intrinsically
since he bore in his soul the image of the divine nature. To
this supernatural endowment of soul God added other gifts.
These are called preternatural for while they are not precisely supernatural, i.e., beyond and above the level of
human nature, they are, nevertheless, a special undeserved
gift of God. Among these gifts were immortality of body
and freedom from sorrow, pain, toil, and infirmity. Added
to these was the wonderful order in man's nature whereby
the inferior part was completely and submissively subject to
the higher, rational faculties; as a consequence he was free
from all inclination to sensuality properly so called. Neither
was there any conflict in him between nature and supernature; both were in complete harmony. All the rest of visible
creation was completely subject to man. So long as the spirit

of man remained subservient to God, both his own nature and nature outside of him remained subject to man.

Moreover God's especial care extended to man's original abode which, corresponding to his eminent endowments, was a "paradise," a garden of delights. Man was to "dress [cultivate] it, and to keep it" (Gen. 2:15). From these words we may infer a divine command to promote culture. In cheerful, not laborious work, men were to subject the earth and the forces in nature: "Fill the earth and subdue it" (Gen. 1:28). They were to develop the created earth which had come from the hand of God not yet fully developed; they were to become collaborators with God.[1] Out of this happy and innocent state man, without dying, was to enter eternal life, and there to enjoy the final and perpetual beatific vision. Man was to earn this destiny, which surpasses the claims of every created nature since it is the happiness of God peculiar to Himself, by his filial subjection to God. To this end, God had given man in paradise a command that, if kept, would have made him forever happy.

2. THE SIN OF ADAM

Man was put to a test. The devil, one of the angels who had fallen through pride and who was the first creature to rebel against the Creator, approached man in the guise of a serpent.[2] With great cunning he persuaded man that the divine command was excessively rigorous, in fact, unjust; that by such a command God was depriving man of a great blessing, namely, *the knowledge of good and evil* (power to

---

[1] Because of Adam's sin work became laborious and oftentimes futile. However, the original purpose of God's command remains.

[2] Because man's mental or spiritual activities are contained within the framework of the sensible, God permitted the devil to tempt man under a guise which was a symbol of his (the devil's) own furtive wickedness.

distinguish between good and evil). Thus tempted, man desired to decide for himself what was good and what was evil, and not to rely upon another for that knowledge, and so he yielded to persuasion. He trespassed the command of God and sinned through pride and disobedience. It is precisely this pride and disobedience that gives rise to the disobedient and false relation between creature and Creator. Pride is a denial of the relations that should ordinarily exist between Creator and creature; the complete dependence of the latter upon the former demands recognition, and this is refused through pride. Therein lies the dishonorable, mendacious, unnatural character of pride and disobedience. He who resists the divine life in the name of nature despoils nature itself. In this sense also is Christ's word true: "For he who would save his life will lose it; but he who loses his life for my sake will save it" (Luke 9:24).

With original sin the eyes of men were opened, but not in the manner expected. It was for them a terrible awakening which made them aware of the wide rift they had caused in nature and of the vast chasm they had opened between God and the world. They realized that now discord had entered their own being, that there was a revolt of sensuality within them, and there was a disturbance of nature about them. In all this they recognized the anger of God, and fear fell upon them. At once their intellect became clouded, for they sought to hide themselves from God. God now pronounced judgment upon sinful creature and meted out condemnation first to the tempter and then to man. Man's life was from that moment to be filled with misery, and, more to the point, he was now subject to death, both spiritual death, i.e., estrangement from God terminating in eternal damnation, and, as its sensible expression, bodily death, i.e., the inescapable doom of those "born of dust." In the same moment, however, the Creator, again revealing His great mercy, promised the sinful race a Redeemer, to be born of a woman, who was to break the power of evil, although He would suffer at the hands of the enemy.

3. ORIGINAL SIN

By his sin the first man did not damage himself alone. Adam, as the Council of Trent (1545–63) teaches, also lost sanctity and justice for us, and brought upon the entire human race sin, spiritual death, and in its train, bodily death, sorrow, misery, and temptation. According to the same Council the bond by which the fatal sin of Adam is transmitted to us is the propagation of the race. How propagation can transmit sin is, and will remain, one of the mysteries of faith that we can never fully comprehend. According to St. Thomas Aquinas, all the descendants of Adam may be considered as so many limbs of *one* body. Just as the action of some member of the body, say the hand, shares in the decision of the will to do something good or evil, with the result that this action becomes either a good deed or a sin, so all members of the human race share in the sin of Adam. This is because he moves them by the act of generation (good in itself because ordained by God) much as the will moves the members of the body. According to St. Augustine, Adam is, as it were, the root out of which mankind springs forth. If the root be corrupted, corruption affects the entire plant.

But we must realize and remember that it is not a sinful *deed* but the *state* of sin that is transmitted. When a man has committed a sin, the state of sin obtains in him until such time as he makes amends for his sinful act by sincere sentiments of repentance. There remains in him, so to speak, an affirmation of his past deed: "If as yet I had not done it, I would do so now." This affirmative tendency of his will abides with the sinner until he wrests from himself a *conversion* of his will that will repudiate the sin committed. Likewise, after Adam had sinned there remained in him an attitude, a state of rebellion against God, i.e., an inclination toward evil.

The correction of the will and the adjustment of it toward the good, toward God, in general can be accomplished only by sanctifying grace. The loss of sanctifying grace entails an inclination toward sin, or at least, the absence of that full surrender which God requires if He is to love man as His child. Now man is born into the world without sanctifying grace, without the habitual inclination of the will to good, without the gifts originally intended for him. Owing to original sin, there is in man a decided tendency toward evil and a certain consent to the rebellion against God first perpetrated by Adam. Hence there is a coresponsibility of all Adam's descendants for the sin of their first parent: "Through one man sin entered into the world and through sin death, and thus death has passed into all men because all have sinned" (Rom. 5:12), i.e., because all have sinned in Adam. From this "inherited sin" result suffering and pain, death and rebellion of the lower instincts against the higher and nobler ones, disturbance in our eternal harmony and balance, and war with nature around us. The sentence of death pronounced upon the first man applies to the entire race descending from him.

A tragic consequence of this proneness to evil is the fact that original sin inevitably gives to all men, or at least to all adults without the powerful aid of God, occasion to commit actual mortal sin. As a matter of fact then, all men would have been liable to eternal damnation, had not God provided a Redeemer. St. Augustine expresses this truth in terrifying words:[3] "By his own personal sin Adam contaminated also his progeny down to the very root, as it were, and exposed them to eternal death and damnation; this is true to the extent that all his descendants have contracted original sin. On this account they were destined, after much aimless striving and pain, to be consigned to eternal punishment, together with their seducers, the apostate angels. 'Through one man sin entered into the world, and through sin death, and so death passed into all men, because all have sinned.' Such was the condition of the human race; all humanity under sentence of eternal perdition lay, indeed, even wallowed in evil, and plunged from sin to sin. And together with the angels who had sinned, it expiated its impious revolt against God" (Enchiridion, No. 26). The condition of the human race in the state of original sin, the clouding of the human intellect, the divine wrath, are all graphically depicted by St. Paul in the following words: "For the wrath of God is revealed from heaven against all ungodliness and wickedness of those men who in wickedness hold back the truth of God . . . seeing that although they know God, they did not glorify him as God or give thanks, but became vain in their reasonings, and their senseless minds have been darkened. For while professing to be wise, they have become fools, and they have changed the glory of the incorruptible God for an image made like to corruptible man and . . . beasts. . . . Therefore God has given them up in the lustful desires of their heart to uncleanness so that they dis-

[3] This passage is read in the breviary and thus has the special approval of the Church.

honor their own bodies among themselves — they who exchanged the truth of God for a lie, and worshiped and served the creature rather than the Creator. . . . For this cause God delivered them up to shameful lusts . . . receiving in themselves the fitting recompense of their perversity" (Rom. 1:18–27).

Our nature is no longer what it was when first it came from the hands of the Creator. Although not essentially corrupted, it was damaged (*homo spoliatus in supernaturalibus, vulneratus in naturalibus*), and has ever since been rebelling against supernature. Though dark the picture is not hopeless. Original sin is the dark background upon which God painted the bright picture of the Redemption. Rising above all the terrors of original sin is the victorious conviction: We have a Redeemer. St. Paul experienced within himself the results of original sin, but he knew nonetheless who could redeem him: "But I see another law in my members, warring against the law of my mind. . . . Unhappy man that I am. Who will deliver me from the body of this death? The grace of God through Jesus Christ, our Lord" (Rom. 7:23–25).

CHAPTER V

REDEMPTION

1. THE REDEEMER

DIVINE and human nature, hitherto separated by not only an essential difference but also by the chasm of sin, were to be reunited for eternity. The creature had opposed itself to the Creator and in so doing had merited for the human race punishment and death. Mankind was rejected and repelled from close communion with God. To atone for the enormity of the sin (man himself could not) and to fulfill the death penalty, as well as to reconcile and reunite God and man, the Son of God chose to become man. In this way, God and man were reunited, for the God-Man, as a member of the offending race, could and did render a worthy and condign satisfaction for man's infinite offense. The death sentence could and would be executed upon Him; yet He, the immortal God-Man, would overthrow death.

Man received the great favor of redemption because God had adopted him as His child and had given him a share in the sonship of His only-begotten Son. Therefore, it was *appropriate* that the Son of God, the Second Person in the Holy Trinity, should become man. And since satisfaction can be rendered only to another, it is obvious that the Son should make satisfaction to the Father. Thus we see that the doctrine of the Redemption has its roots in that of the Holy Trinity. The "mission" of the Son of God in the world is a continuation of His eternal procession from the Father. We see also how closely our redemption is linked with the God-Man. This God-Man who, as we have said above, was the center of God's original design of the universe, is our Lord *Jesus Christ*.

That Christ is truly God is evident from His own testimony. During the Feast of the Dedication of the Temple, in the middle of December, when cloudbursts were of frequent occurrence, the Lord was walking in the covered portico called "Solomon's Porch" within the outer temple court. There the Jews crowded around Him and asked: "How long dost thou keep us in suspense? If thou art the Christ [the Anointed, the Redeemer foretold by the prophets], tell us openly." Jesus answered that He had already told them so, often and plainly. Had they been willing, they would have believed in Him long ago. And He concluded with the words: "I and the Father are one" (John 10:22–30). At these words the Jews picked up stones to kill Him. They understood full well that He deemed Himself equal to God, but as usual they interpreted His claim as blasphemy, a crime which, according to Jewish Law, was punishable with death by stoning. Again, when the Apostle St. Philip at the Last Supper voiced the somewhat imprudent request: "Lord, show us the Father," He replied: "Have I been so long a time with you, and you have not known me? Philip, he who sees me sees also the Father. . . . Dost thou not believe that I am in the Father and the Father in me?" (John 14:8–10.) The same truth is evinced by His claim to forgive sins in His *own* name, which the Jews again rightly understood. Thus, when a paralytic was let down through the roof into a house where Jesus happened to be, He said to him: "Son, thy sins are forgiven thee." The scribes, who would not accept Christ's Messianic claims, thought within themselves: "Why does this man speak thus? He blasphemes. Who can forgive sins, but God only?" And Jesus, knowing their thoughts, said, "Why do you harbor evil thoughts in your hearts? For which is easier, to say, 'Thy sins are forgiven thee,' or to say, 'Arise, and walk?' But that you may know that the Son of Man has power on earth to forgive sins," he then said to the paralytic, "Arise, take up thy pallet and go to thy house." He adopts their way of thinking for a moment, as it were, and says: "Surely, God alone can forgive sins. But I have shown you by a miracle that I have such power and therefore am God" (Mark 2:1–12; Matt. 9:1–8; Luke 5:17–26). Finally we quote the beautiful words of Christ which express the equality of the Son with His heavenly Father: "I praise thee, Father, Lord of heaven and earth, that thou didst hide these things from the wise and prudent, and didst reveal them to little ones. Yes, Father, for such was thy good pleasure. All things have been delivered to me by my Father; and no one knows the Son except the Father; nor does anyone know the Father except the Son, and him to whom the Son chooses to reveal him" (Matt. 11:25–27 and Luke 10:21–22).

By such and numerous other utterances the Redeemer proves that He is the one of whom Isaias had prophesied: "For a child is born to us, and a son is given to us, and the government is upon his shoulder: and his name shall be called, Wonderful, Counsellor, *God,* Mighty, the Father of the world to come, the Prince of peace" (Isa. 9:6), and whom, seven or eight centuries before His birth, he had called Emmanuel, i.e., God with us (Isa. 7:14). This dogma of faith, for which countless martyrs shed their blood, was defined against the error of Arius by the General Council of Nice (325), which professed, as we still do in the Creed at Mass, that He is "God of God, Light of Light, true God of true God, born not made, of the same substance as the Father."

Our faith teaches us that the "Son of God" took human form in the womb of the Virgin Mary. He appears on earth as a real man: He eats and sleeps and is fatigued by travel. His human nature becomes most evident on Mount Olivet, where He experiences the very natural revulsion of His human will against death and is overcome by the fearful dread of it, although He at once subjects that will to the will of His heavenly Father: "Father, if it is possible, let this cup pass away from me; yet not as I will, but as Thou willest" (Matt. 26:39). Yes, Christ chose to become man, to be one of us, to be born even as we are, and thus to become a member of our race. He willed to be a divine paradox by coming forth a Redeemer from the fallen race itself, an Expiator from the offending race.

Accordingly, there are *two natures* in Christ, the divine and the human, and these two natures are united in one person. "The word was made flesh" (John 1:14). This is the hypostatic union, i.e., a union in person; in other words, *one Person* with *two natures*. In order to have a clear idea of person and nature, the following observations might be kept in mind. We can make different statements about Christ, a few of which we arrange in the following scheme:

Christ is born 1
Christ is eternal 2
Christ died 1
Christ is immutable 2
Christ is Creator of the world 2

We readily perceive that some of these statements agree and others apparently contradict. Those in agreement are marked with the same number, those in contradiction with opposite numbers. Obviously then, we can divide all assertions made of Christ into two categories, each necessarily having its respective source or principle of action. The source of, or the reason for, the assertions which can be made of any person is called the nature (i.e., essence considered as the principle of activity).

He of whom these assertions are made is called the person. Essence answers the question: *What* is it? Person answers the question: *Who* is it? We may, therefore, define person and essence as follows: (1) person (in rational beings) is that of which something is predicated or asserted; it is the bearer of the attributes of the being; (2) essence or nature, on the other hand, is that by virtue of which one may make an assertion — it is the totality, the source of the attributes. He who is accountable for an act is the person; that in virtue of which the act is performed is the nature. Christ is eternal in virtue of His *divine* nature; He died in virtue of His *human nature*. In Christ the divine and human natures are united in *one divine* person, one Ego. God became man; He that was God from all eternity assumed a human nature in time, and hence is at the same time God and man. Based on this truth is our right to predicate human things of God and divine things of man, e.g., God died on the cross.

This doctrine was upheld and defined in three General Councils against two heresies. First, the heretic Nestorius, patriarch of Constantinople, asserted that Mary was not the Mother of God, but that she had given birth to a human being whom God had subsequently endowed with exceptional sanctity or grace. Against him, St. Cyril, patriarch of

Alexandria, championed the true doctrine, and the third General Council (431), that of Ephesus, declared Mary to be the Mother of God. The Archimandrite (approximately Abbot) Eutyches of Constantinople, on the other hand, asserted that Christ was not a real man; that His divine nature had absorbed his humanity (Monophysitism). To combat this error Pope Leo the Great (d. 461) convoked the General Council of Chalcedon (451) and was represented there by a legate. When a letter of the pope clearly stating the doctrine of the two natures in Christ was read before the assembled council, the Fathers present exclaimed: "That is the faith of the Fathers, the faith of the Apostles: Thus we believe: Peter has spoken through Leo." Finally, at the Council of Constantinople (553), the term "hypostatic union" was coined.

We might now ask what are the consequences of the union of the two natures in Christ Himself? The human nature of Christ participates in the divine Sonship, so that He who dwelt among men, as we do, is the Son of God. As such He has a claim upon the heritage of the Son of God, which consists above all in the paternal Love of God, i.e., the Holy Spirit. God the Father communicates His Spirit to the humanity of Christ; and indeed this communication is no longer an unmerited grace, for Christ has a rightful claim to it, being the natural Son of God. The Holy Spirit pours out the fullness of grace[1] over the human nature of Christ and stamps upon it a perfect image of Himself as far as that is possible. For we must realize that while in and of itself the hypostatic union requires it, it does not effect the elevation of Christ's *human soul* and its faculties into participation in

---

[1] Properly speaking, the word "grace" does not suit, for this deification of Christ's human nature is no gratuitous grace, but the heritage to which Christ has a right even as man.

the divine nature. Sanctifying grace must first enter into the human soul of Christ and thus raise it far beyond the human level, beyond the realm of created being, and make it God-like. Since sanctifying grace is, as it were, an emanation and image of the Holy Spirit, the Fathers of the Church frequently speak of sanctification as "unction of the Holy Spirit." St. Cyril, whom we have quoted on several occasions, and who, together with Pope Leo the Great, seems to have been singled out by Divine Providence to penetrate deeply into the mystery of the God-Man, says of Christ: "As man He also was anointed and sanctified; as true God, however, in so far as He proceeds from the Father, He directly sanctifies His own Temple (His humanity) with His own Spirit (the Holy Spirit) and through this humanity sanctifies all creatures" (St. Cyril Alex. on John 11:11).

The same doctrine may be stated as follows. Through the fact of the hypostatic union with the divinity, the human nature of Christ is *objectively* holy while its *subjective* sanctity is a *consequence* of this union. Christ therefore possesses sanctifying grace (by way of participation of His human soul in the divine nature) in the greatest fullness, so that His human nature, as the instrument of His divinity, can become in its turn the cause of our sanctification through sanctifying grace. "I beheld the Spirit descending as a dove from heaven, and it abode upon him. And I did not know him. But he who sent me to baptize with water said to me, 'He upon whom thou wilt see the Spirit descending, and abiding upon him, he it is who baptizes with the Holy Spirit'" (John 1:32-33).

Through His Incarnation, the Son of God became also the natural mediator between God and man. "For," writes St. Paul, "there is one God, and one mediator between God and men, himself man, Christ Jesus" (I Tim. 2:5). Thus Christ is by nature *the* High Priest; by the fact of incarnation He was consecrated *the* Priest. Whoever else calls himself priest does so only because his priesthood has some reference to Christ (in the Old Testament and to some extent even among heathens), or because, sharing in Christ's priesthood, he takes the place of Christ (priests of the New Testament). St. Paul elucidates this for us in his Epistle to the Hebrews: "Having therefore a great high priest who has passed into the heavens, Jesus the Son of God, let us hold fast our confession. For we have not a high priest who cannot have compassion on our infirmities, but one tried as we are in all things except sin" (Heb. 4:14–15). "For every high priest taken from among men is appointed for men in the things pertaining to God, that he may offer gifts and sacrifices for sins. He is able to have compassion on the ignorant and erring, because he himself is also beset with weakness. . . . And no man takes the honor to himself; he takes it who is called by God as Aaron was" (Heb. 5:1–4). These two conditions, i.e., that he be taken from among men and have compassion on them, and that he be called by God, were fulfilled in the person of Jesus. "So also Christ did not glorify himself with the high priesthood, but he who spoke to him, 'Thou art my Son, I this day have begotten thee.' . . . For Jesus in the days of his earthly life, with a loud cry and tears [especially on Mount Olivet], offered up prayers and supplications to him who was able to save him from death, and was heard because of his reverent submission. And he, Son though he was, learned obedience from the things that he suffered; and when perfected, he became to all who obey him the cause of eternal salvation, called by God a high priest according to the order of Melchisedech" (Heb. 5:5–10).

Where there is a priest, there must also be a sacrifice. In the third section of this chapter we shall see how Christ, the High Priest, offered his sacrifice. But first we will speak of Mary, the Mother of God, who cooperated so decisively in the Incarnation, and of Joseph who was her faithful companion and the foster father of Christ.

2. THE MOTHER OF THE REDEEMER

It is significant that the Catholic people rose in protest against the heresy of Nestorius from the very moment that he began to assail Mary's divine maternity. Indeed Christianity has most intimately identified itself with this mystery. The mystery of the union of the divine nature with the human nature in one divine Person is most strikingly revealed in the formula: "Mary is the Mother of God; Mary has given birth to God." The divine maternity of Mary was solemnly proclaimed at the General Council of Ephesus (431), from which time also the building of churches under her patronage received a new impetus, e.g., the Church of St. Mary Major in Rome. Her divine maternity is the source of all the prerogatives that Catholics recognize in her.

The first of her prerogatives is perpetual virginity. That she was a virgin before and after the birth of Christ and that she purposed to remain ever after a virgin, is evident beyond all doubt from her reply to the Angel Gabriel: "How shall this happen, since I do not know man?" (Luke 1:34.) That she persevered spotless in her virginity is plain from these same words, for it is inconceivable that after giving birth to the Son of God she should have abandoned her purpose. The same is evident from the fact that shortly before His death on the cross, Christ gave the Apostle St. John to her as a son and committed him to her care. He said to Mary: "Woman, behold thy son!" (John 19:26), and to John: "Behold thy mother!" (John 19:27.)

Therefore the Church has from earliest times kept inviolate her faith in the perpetual virginity of Mary. Only Tertullian, the eminent ecclesiastical writer who lapsed into heresy, and Helvidius and Jovinian, other heretics, dared to question the doctrine. The "brethren" of Jesus, whom Scripture mentions, were merely cousins. Abraham called his nephew Lot his "brother" (Gen. 14:14), because it was formerly the custom to speak of relatives as brethren or sisters and the Hebrew language had no word for "nephew." The apostle St. James the Less and his brother Joseph, spoken of as brethren of Jesus, were the sons of a certain Mary. Of her we read in John (19:25) that she was with the women who stood at the foot of the cross, and is there called "sister" of the Mother of God and wife of Cleophas or Alphaeus. According to a tradition, of which Hegesippus (d. 180), and St. Jerome (d. 419 or 420) are witnesses, Alphaeus was a brother of St. Joseph. Hence this Mary was a sister-in-law of the Mother of God and her sons the cousins of Jesus.

The full spiritual, supernatural beauty of her who was selected to enter so deeply into the mystery of the Incarnation of the Son of God is particularly brought out in the dogma of the Immaculate Conception proclaimed on December 8, 1854, by Pope Pius IX. Mary, the Mother of God, from the very instant of her conception (in the womb of her mother Anna) was, in virtue of the merits of Christ, preserved from the stain of original sin. This doctrine is also clearly contained in tradition, and implicitly stated in Holy Scripture.[2] The Fathers of the Church never wearied of prais-

---

[2] The dogma of the Immaculate Conception is implied (1) in the so-called "proto-Gospel" (Gen. 3:15), where God put enmity between the serpent and *the* woman; and (2) in the words of the angel: "Thou art *full* of grace."

ing the purity and sanctity of the Mother of God, comparing
her to Eve before the fall, yet extolling her high above the
mother of our race. One of the first to chant her praises was
St. Ephraem the Syrian (d. 373). In his *Nisibenian Hymns*
(27:8) he represents the church of Edessa as thus addressing
the Lord: "Thou alone and Thy Mother are beautiful
beyond all. There is no stain in Thee and no fault in Thy
Mother: to which of these two beautiful beings can I com-
pare my children?" During the Middle Ages difficulties were
raised regarding this doctrine, because some feared that it
disparaged the efficacy of the Redemption through Christ.
The Franciscan theologian John Duns Scotus (d. 1308)
sought to solve the difficulty by saying that Mary was redeemed by a more perfect act of redemption than we; she
was exempted from original sin in view of the redemption
to be accomplished by Christ. Divine Providence, however,
disposed things in such wise that here not so much the wisdom of theologians but the plain, living faith of the people
was decisive. The Feast of the Immaculate Conception was
celebrated in the East as early as the *seventh* century, and in
the West since the *ninth* century. During the ensuing centuries the popes repeatedly prohibited statements derogatory
to this truth. Finally, in view of its acceptance by universal
Christendom, Pope Pius IX solemnly proclaimed it as *de
fide*. (The bodily assumption of Mary into heaven is also a
universal teaching of the Church, as is witnessed by her
feast of August 15.)

The Mother of God holds a singular position in the
economy of the Redemption, and consequently exercises an
important function in our religious life. As Mother of Christ
she is also *our* Mother for we are members of the Body of
Christ. God had, in a measure, conditioned the work of our

redemption on her consent and willingness to be the Mother of the one who was to be despised by men and to die on the cross. She gave her consent: "Behold the handmaid of the Lord; be it done to me according to thy word" (Luke 1:38). Thus she became the coadjutrix in the work of Redemption, the Deaconess of Christ's great sacrifice, by bearing Him and co-offering Him upon the cross. She became our Mother by bringing us forth in sorrow at the foot of the cross. This also forms the basis for the views of recent popes that Mary is intercessory mediatrix and stewardess of all graces. We emphasize the word "intercessory" for Christ will always remain the sole Mediator between God and man. But Mary, as Mother of Christ and our Mother, beseeches Christ to bring us into union with Him and from this motherly solicitude of Mary no one is excluded.

The Fathers of the Church often refer to Mary as the *second Eve*. Just as the first Eve handed the forbidden fruit to the first Adam and cooperated in the condemnation of the world, so this second Eve delivered to the second Adam the blessed fruit of her holy body and co-operated in the redemption of the world.

By her humble submission to God and His holy will, Mary became the prototype of religion, i.e., of the attitude of the creature to the Creator. "In the humble *'fiat'* [be it done], with which she replied to the Angel, rests the mystery of redemption, considered on the part of the creature. For toward his redemption man has nothing to contribute but the willingness of unconditional submission" (Gertrude von Le Fort).

From all that has been said, it is evident that Mary is entitled to a very special and singular veneration called *hyperdulia*, which Christians have paid her throughout the centuries. Indeed Mary seems to have foreseen this devotion, for in the *Magnificat* she sings: "Henceforth all generations shall call me blessed" (Luke 1:48), a thought we repeat daily at Vespers. The first one to honor Mary was her cousin Elizabeth, mother of John the Baptist. When Mary came to visit her, Elizabeth exclaimed: "Blessed art thou among women and blessed is the fruit of thy womb! And how have I deserved that the mother of my Lord should come to me?" (Luke 1:42.) These words, together with those of the angel Gabriel, make up the "Hail Mary," a prayer which has been repeated innumerable times ever since by the faithful of all places and ages. The oldest churches erected in her honor date from the fourth century; the oldest feast, that of her Dormition (to use the Latin expression still employed by the Greek Church), called today the Assumption, is first mentioned about A.D. 500. The earliest pictures of her are found in the Roman catacombs and date from the second century.

Next to the Blessed Virgin stands *St. Joseph,* the guardian and foster father of the Lord. Because he lived in legal wedlock with Mary, he is legally the father of Jesus. If we recall what importance the Israelites attached to all legal matters,[3] we will readily understand that St. Joseph was much more than a mere foster father. For this reason, St. Matthew presents the genealogy of Joseph as that of Christ (1:1–17).[4] Because Mary with Joseph was a descendant of David,

---

[3] Thus the brother of an Israelite who died without issue had to marry his dead brother's wife. The first-born son of this union bore the name of the deceased and was considered his legal offspring. In this way the genealogy of no family could come to an end before the birth of the Messias.

[4] According to many commentators, the genealogy given by St. Luke (3:23-38) is that of the Blessed Virgin, but according to others, it is that of St. Joseph. Its difference from the genealogy given by St. Matthew is explained by the legal marriage of St. Joseph's father. St. Matthew records the natural father of St. Joseph, while St. Luke records the "legal" father.

Christ both in fact and in law was, according to official gen-
ealogical records, a descendant of King David[5] whose scion,
as promised, the Saviour was to be.

3. THE REDEMPTIVE ACT

The Son of God came upon earth to satisfy for Adam's
sinful deed with its so fatal consequences. Since by disobedience Adam had altogether denied his surrender and
submission to God's Will, by a most perfect act of obedience
Christ would substitute and sacrifice Himself in man's stead
to appease the wrath of God.

Christ's entire life was consecrated to the task: "I am not
come to do my will, but the will of Him that sent Me."
Obedience to His heavenly Father was the invisible food He
spoke of to the disciples (John 4:32). This aim would be
actualized in a deed manifesting His obedience before the
eyes of men. As decreed eternally by the Father, this should
come to pass in the offering of Himself as a sacrifice upon the
cross. The Sacrifice is the external act in which the surrender of the Son of God to his Father is embodied. Being
the atonement of Adam's sin it is a sacrifice of pain, and it
was designed from all eternity by God for the redemption of
mankind. To fulfill it, the eternal High Priest came into
the world.[6] Thus Christ is both sacrificing priest and sacrificial victim.

In Christ's person, the sentence of death, which God had
pronounced upon the human race, was executed. "The

[5] The Davidic descent of Mary can be deduced perhaps from St. Luke
(1:26–27): "The angel Gabriel was sent . . . to a Virgin betrothed to a man
whose name was Joseph, of the house of David." Some commentators refer
the words "of the house of David" to the antecedent "virgin."

[6] Christ's sacrifice is the prototype of every sacrifice. The essence of sacrifice,
which is the offering of a visible gift to God in order to acknowledge and
adore Him as the supreme Lord, is exemplified by it.

Saviour has suffered and 'reconciled all things, whether on the earth or in the heavens, making peace through the blood of his cross' (Col. 1:20). For we were enemies of God through sin, and God had sentenced the sinners to death. Now, of two things, one had to be done: Either God would abide by His sentence and destroy all men, or He would be merciful and repeal the sentence. But behold His wisdom: He upheld justice and yet showed mercy. Christ 'bore our sins in his body upon the tree [of the cross], that we, having died to sin, through his death might live unto justice'" (I Pet. 2:24) (St. Cyril of Jerusalem, Catechesis 13:33). Because Life itself died, death was overcome and destroyed.

The sacrifice of the cross is the most sublime act of the worship of God. By it the world fulfills its destiny, to give God highest honor through Jesus Christ. St. Paul speaks at length of this sacrifice in his Epistle to the Hebrews. He first speaks of the sacrifices of the Old Law once offered in the sanctuary. He describes the Tabernacle of the Covenant, or the Temple where the "Holy" was. "Beyond the second veil was the tabernacle which is called the Holy of Holies. . . . But of all these we cannot now speak in detail. Such then being the arrangements, the priests always used to enter into the first tabernacle to perform the sacred rites; but into the second tabernacle the high priest alone entered once a year, not without blood, which he offered for his own and the people's sins of ignorance" (Heb. 9:3-7). All this St. Paul sees as foreshadowing the real Sanctuary, i.e., heaven, closed so long as the Old Covenant remained in force. The sacrifices of the Old Law were powerless to purify conscience and to effect really interior justification. They were but types foreshadowing the reality eventually accomplished by Christ. Therefore these sacrifices had to be repeated constantly for no one of them could suffice. Over against all these imperfect sacrifices was set the one perfect sacrifice, offered by Christ. He entered the true Holy of Holies "not made by human hands . . . [i.e. heaven], nor again by virtue of blood of goats and calves, but by virtue of his own blood; into the Holies, having obtained eternal redemption" (Heb. 9:12). Since the blood of the God-Man can bring about real expiation and internal justification, His sacrifice was not repeated. He has offered it once for all, reopening heaven thereby. Hence, "He is mediator of a new covenant" (Heb. 9:15). Neither was it necessary for Him to "offer himself often, as the high priest enters into the Holies year after year with blood not his own: for in that case he must have suffered often. . . . But as it is, once for all at the end of the ages, he has appeared for the destruction of sin by the sacrifice of himself" (Heb. 9:25–26).

At the price of His own blood, Christ delivered us from the power of the devil. He, our substitute, assumed the punishment due to sin and suffered the death penalty due us. He destroyed death for He is life itself. He offered an adequate and condign satisfaction. As says St. Anselm of Canterbury (d. 1109), Christ alone could do it, for only a human being could expiate the sin of man; only a God could satisfy the justice of a God; and only a God-Man could overthrow death.

According to Catholic teaching, Christ died for *all* men including those who lived under the Old Law. The just of the Old Law were compelled to remain in an intermediate state, Limbo, until the redemption had been accomplished.[7]

<hr>

[7] The application of the fruits of the Redemption to the just of the Old Law took place during that mysterious descent of Christ into "hell" (I Pet. 3:19–20).

Christ "is a propitiation for our sins, not for ours only but also for those of the whole world" (I John 2:2). The Church condemns as heretical all teachings that would limit the benefits of the Christ's death to a privileged class of man (e.g., the doctrine of Calvin and of Jansenius, according to whom Christ died only for the "Predestinate"). The Church has always insisted upon the universality of the Redemption and upon God's will to save all men: "who wishes all men to be saved" (I Tim. 2:4). The actual realization of the Redemption by the individual depends, however, upon the consent of man, which consent he is free to withhold. The Redemption by Christ is absolutely perfect and superabundant; He made reparation beyond measure for the harm done by Adam. According to the teaching of St. Paul (Rom. 5) the grace flowing to us from the Redemption far outweighs the loss that has come to us as our inheritance from Adam. For this reason the Church sings on Holy Saturday, during the blessing of the Paschal candle: "O happy fault that merited so great and so exalted a Redeemer!" God permitted original sin, only because He foreknew what wonderful things He was to accomplish in Christ.

4. THE RISEN REDEEMER

But with the death of Christ our Redemption was not completed. The sin of Adam would not have harmed if he had not been our common progenitor from whom we inherited original sin; so the act of reparation, the obedience of Christ, could not have benefited us if we were not in some way His "children" by an intimate bond through which we could inherit justification. For this end Christ chose to *rise from the dead* and take possession of His glorified life in heaven, so as to become one with us in order to apply the

Redemption to us. This is a matter of the greatest significance. It shows us that Easter, not Good Friday, is the chief feast of our Redemption. Only by the Resurrection of the God-Man was the death of sin overthrown.

The merits of Christ are imputed to us not merely externally or extrinsically, but internally and intrinsically; we are to have an intrinsic share in them.[8] "The Lord cured the disobedience on the tree through obedience upon the tree. By the first Adam we offended God in not observing His commandment. By the Second Adam we were reconciled with Him, made obedient unto death" (Irenaeus, Adversus Haereses 5, 16, 3). As from Adam we inherited aversion to God and inclination toward evil, so, too, we inherited from Christ conversion to, and love for, God, i.e., the condition of sonship. Something in the Redemption must parallel our carnal descent from Adam. This something must be more spiritual since the effect it produces will be more spiritual, more divine. The Lord Himself calls it a spiritual regeneration, a birth from the spirit, in contrast to our birth from the flesh, from Adam. When Nicodemus inquired of Him the conditions for entering the Kingdom of God, Christ answered: "Amen, Amen, I say to thee, unless a man be born again of water and the Spirit, he cannot enter into the kingdom of God. That which is born of the flesh is flesh; and that which is born of the Spirit is spirit" (John 3:5–6). He speaks here plainly of *Baptism* as a rebirth from the Spirit. This rebirth implies our descent from Christ, and is the means of applying to us the merits of His Redemption. This union with Christ, this baptism in Him, causes His own justice,

[8] This doctrine marks the chief difference between Catholicism and Lutheranism. According to Luther, the merits of Christ are imputed to us only externally; because of these merits God overlooks our ever persistent state of sin. Obviously then, the principal feast of the Protestants is Good Friday.

His own holiness, to flow in us. Everyone, therefore, must be spiritually reborn of Christ and enter into union with Him.

To effect this the Redeemer must live and that life must be different from His life upon earth. It was necessary then for Him to take possession of His glorified life after the Resurrection and Ascension, in order that He might unite Himself with, and communicate His *glorified life* to, us. Thus He told His disciples before the Ascension: "I will not leave you orphans; I will come to you. Yet a little while and the world no longer sees me. But you see me, for I live and you shall live. . . . I go away and I am coming to you" (John 14:18, 19, 28). Christ becomes the second, the "spiritual," Adam (I Cor. 15:45), the second progenitor of the human race, but He is an Adam far more perfect than the first one. Through personal contact with Himself and His redemptive work in the sacrament of baptism He begets each one into a new life born of God. In the fifth chapter of his Epistle to the Romans, St. Paul draws a parallel between Adam and Christ and offers us one of the most profound and fundamental passages in the entire New Testament: "As through one man sin entered into the world and through sin death, and thus death has passed into all men because all have sinned . . . as from the offense of the one man the result was unto condemnation to all men, so from the justice of the one the result is unto justification of life to all men. For just as by the disobedience of the one man the many were constituted sinners, so also by the obedience of the one the many will be constituted just" (Rom. 5:12, 18, 19). According to St. Paul, there is but one difference, that of *measure*. Christ gave us much more than Adam lost for us: "Much more has the grace of God, and the gift in the grace of the one man Jesus Christ, abounded unto the many"

(Rom. 5:15). This gift of God is called "the abundance of the grace and of the gift of justice" (Rom. 5:17). "Where the offense has abounded, grace has abounded yet more" (Rom. 5:20). Thus Adam was not only an antitype, but also a proto-type of Christ. Christ is the true progenitor of the redeemed race.

This whole doctrine lies deep at the heart of Christianity and may be represented graphically thus:

The obedience of Christ		The disobedience of Adam
The spiritual rebirth out of Christ (baptism)	is greater than	The carnal descent from Adam
Inherited justice		Original sin

We can perceive now more clearly how our Redemption was completed only by the Resurrection of Christ. "If Christ has not risen, vain is your faith, for you are still in your sins" (I Cor. 15:17). The Redemption was to be imparted to us. But to this end Christ must live, be glorified, and lead that higher life into which He entered by His Resurrection and Ascension. He imparts Himself to us in baptism and in the other sacraments and impels us to enter into His Redemption. He not only satisfied *for* us as our substitute, but desires to do so *within* us. We are justified not solely by an extrinsic imputation of Christ's merits (while remaining intrinsically sinful as before), but we are justified intrinsically and truly become just and holy because the merits of Christ abound in us.

Christ "was delivered up for our sins and rose again for our justification" (Rom. 4:25). By His Resurrection alone could our justification be consummated. The Redeemer became the head of the body of which we are the members;

became the vine of which we are the branches. "I am the true vine, and my Father is the vine dresser. Every branch in me that bears no fruit he will take away; and every branch that bears forth fruit he will cleanse, that it may bear more fruit. You are already clean because of the word that I have spoken to you. Abide in me, and I in you. As the branch cannot bear fruit of itself unless it remain on the vine, so neither can you unless you abide in me. I am the vine, you are the branches. He who abides in me, and I in him, he bears much fruit; for without me you can do nothing. If anyone does not abide in me, he shall be cast outside as the branch and wither; and they shall gather them up and cast them into the fire, and they shall burn. If you abide in me, and if my words abide in you, ask whatever you will and it shall be done to you. In this is my Father glorified, that you may bear very much fruit, and become my disciples" (John 15:1–8).

We can now proceed to discuss the application of the fruits of the salvation which Christ merited on the cross.

PART III

APPLICATION OF THE REDEMPTION:
OUR SANCTIFICATION

CHAPTER VI

GOD THE SANCTIFIER

1. THE HOLY SPIRIT

THE work of sanctification is generally ascribed to the Holy Spirit, the Third Person of the Blessed Trinity. Since sanctification is, in a way, a new creation, it is the work of all three divine Persons, i.e., of the one God. There are good reasons, however, for calling the Holy Spirit sanctifier in a special manner. To understand why this is so we have only to recall what has been said above concerning Him. To summarize:

The Third Divine Person is the expression of love within the Holy Trinity. He is the bond of love between the Father and the Son, and hence also the bond of unity between the Father and Son as distinct Persons. Since He is the expression of the totality of the holy will of God, he is the expression of God's holiness, the Holy Spirit, the Spirit of Sanctity. He is, if one may so describe Him, the flower of the life of the Holy Trinity. By Him the humanity of Christ was anointed (sanctified); by Him the humanity of Christ is drawn into union with the divine life; and by Him are poured love and sanctity, as the image of Himself, into the human soul of Christ.

How appropriate it was, therefore, that God should bestow

the Holy Spirit upon man, His adoptive son. It was done in order that the Holy Spirit may transform man into His own image, stamp His image upon him, and become his bond of union with God. Hence we are quite right in attributing the infusion of sanctifying grace, i.e., the sanctification of man, to the Holy Spirit. Through him God's love for us is poured out into our hearts, and by Him love for God is infused into our hearts. "The charity of God[1] is poured forth in our hearts by the Holy Spirit who has been given to us" (Rom. 5:5).

2. CHRIST AND THE HOLY SPIRIT

From the above and from what has been said previously, we conclude that a very singular relationship exists between Christ and the Holy Spirit. The Holy Spirit becomes the Spirit of Christ, even according to the human nature of the latter. Even as man, Christ possesses the Holy Spirit as a gift due Him. Since as man Christ is the Son of God through the hypostatic union, He has a claim upon the love of God the Father, and in turn upon the Holy Spirit who is the expression of the love and unity between Father and Son.

The Holy Spirit molds the humanity of Christ after His own image and thereby makes it Godlike. This deification of Christ's humanity manifests itself, first, in the sanctity of His soul, intellect, and will; and, second, in the transfiguration or *glorification* of His entire humanity, even of His body. To this glorification the Son of God made man had a right from the very beginning. But in order to assume the burden of our sins and to accomplish the work of Redemp-

---

[1] According to the context, this passage refers to the love which God bears us. Many of the Church Fathers, however, interpret it as the love which we bear God.

tion in all humility, He laid His glory and majesty aside, as it were, and renounced it during His lifetime. Once only did He choose to show the chosen disciples, Peter, James, and John, the glory which was His by right of title. He took them with Him to Mount Thabor's heights, "And was transfigured before them. And his face shone as the sun, and his garments became white as snow" (Matt. 17:2). God Himself attests the reason for this transfiguration when His voice is heard from heaven, saying: "This is my beloved Son, in whom I am well pleased" (Matt. 17:5). This man, then, standing there in glorious transfiguration, is the Son of God, and truly is the majesty of God due Him.

Although the Saviour, while still on earth, chose to waive His majesty, yet He was to regain it by His death in obedience to the command of the Father. "Who [Christ], though he was by nature God, did not consider being equal to God a thing to be clung to, but emptied himself, taking the nature of a slave and being made like unto men. And appearing in the form of man, he humbled himself, becoming obedient to death, even to death on a cross. Therefore God also has exalted him and has bestowed upon him the name that is above every name, so that at the name of Jesus every knee should bend of those in heaven, on earth and under the earth, and every tongue should confess that the Lord Jesus Christ is in the glory of God the Father" (Phil. 2:6–11). Christ chose to assume the whole burden and responsibility of sinful humanity in order, by His death on the cross, to liberate the entire race of man. He consequently entered into His glory through the gloomy portal of death. This glory became apparent in some measure when after the Resurrection His body possessed certain qualities that ordinary men do not possess. He was subtile like a spirit, a fact which convinced men that His body was spiritualized.[2] This *spiritualization* of Christ's humanity was also the work of the Holy Spirit who was in Him and who had thoroughly permeated the humanity of the Son of God, and entirely spiritualized, even deified it. "The Lord is a spirit" (II Cor. 3:17) says St. Paul, i.e., Christ is wholly spirit and deified, entirely penetrated and transformed by the Holy Spirit who is Christ's own Spirit. The Fathers of the Church illustrate this truth by comparing the human nature of Christ to a piece of iron placed in a fire. Just as the iron eventually becomes fiery without ceasing to be iron, so the humanity of Christ becomes divine without ceasing to be humanity. This glorification so lays hold of Christ that His historical mission, His redemptive acts performed on this earth, enter into glorification and into eternity. In the presence of God they exist eternally.

If we now ask ourselves: "How is the Holy Spirit present to *us*? How can we share in the Holy Spirit?" we soon arrive at a very important and fundamental truth. From what has been said, the answer to our questions can only be: "In Christ, in the glorified humanity of Christ." When we come into contact with the humanity of Christ, the Holy Spirit enters into us. The flame that glows in Christ passes over to him who is in contact with Christ; i.e., he becomes like unto the iron laid in the fire. He, too, shares in the Holy Spirit, the Spirit of Christ, the Son of God; he, too, shares in the sonship of the Incarnate Word of God and is transformed into

[2] Our language is awkward in explaining supernatural realities. If we speak here of "spiritualization," we do not use the word "spirit" in opposition to body, but in opposition to the merely natural and earthly body, subject to the laws of the physical world. The body, therefore, was not subtilized out of existence. As the perfectly molded instrument of a soul inhabited by the Holy Spirit, the body becomes in a true sense the "embodiment" of this soul; the body itself becomes spiritualized.

Him by the Holy Spirit. So Christ's flesh becomes quickening flesh.

It is therefore no longer enigmatic when we find Holy Scripture ascribing certain operations at times to the Holy Spirit and at other times to Christ. They are the operations of the spiritualized Christ, of the Spirit of Christ, of the Spirit in Christ. The Holy Spirit, together with the glorified God-Man, comes and is sent to us in and through Him; this sending of the Holy Spirit coincides with the return of Christ from heaven. The sending of the former is a particular reality distinct from the return of the latter,[3] but these realities are intimately connected with one another and pervade one another. Thus we understand how Christ could say to the disciples: "It is expedient to you that I depart. For if I do not go, the Advocate will not come to you; but if I go, I will send him to you" (John 16:7); and how St. John could write, "For the Spirit had not yet been given, seeing that Jesus had not yet been glorified" (John 7:39). The Pentecostal mystery is the fruit of the Easter mystery; the descent of the Holy Spirit follows the Resurrection and Ascension. Thus St. Peter says: Jesus "exalted by the right hand of God, and receiving from the Father the promise of the Holy Spirit, has poured forth this Spirit, which you see and hear" (Acts 2:33).

3. THE HOLY SPIRIT IN MAN

We have just said that the Holy Spirit, who anoints and sanctifies Christ's humanity, descends upon anyone who is a branch of the vine, i.e., Christ; that whoever is incorporated in Christ is anointed with the Holy Spirit. By incorporation

---

[3] This follows from the fact that the union with Christ can persist, although only externally, if the Holy Spirit abandons man because of sin (see below).

in Christ the creature participates in the Sonship of the God-Man. Consequently there belongs to him also the Spirit of love and unity with which the Father loves the Son. "The charity of God is poured forth in our hearts by the Holy Spirit who has been given to us" (Rom. 5:5). "Because you are sons, God has sent the Spirit of his Son into our hearts, crying 'Abba, Father' " (Gal. 4:6). The Holy Spirit fashions the creature upon whom He rests into the image of the Son of God. He glorifies and deifies every member incorporated in Christ.

Moreover the Holy Spirit is a pledge unto us of eternal glory. In his own good time He will complete the work of glorification in us. Just as He transfigured Christ in eternal bliss, so will He also transfigure us body and soul. In the passage from St. Paul to the Ephesians, which governs the divisions of this book, the Apostle says: "In him (Christ) you too, when you had heard the word of truth, the good news of your salvation, and believed in it, were sealed with the Holy Spirit of the promise, who is the pledge of our inheritance, for a redemption of possession, for the praise of his glory" (Eph. 1:13, 14). The Holy Spirit, when we abide in Christ, is impressed upon us like a seal and is thereby made a pledge to us of eternal glory, the completion of our redemption. The Holy Spirit, then, effects in us a continuous progressive transformation into the image of Christ. "But we all, with faces unveiled, reflecting as in a mirror the glory of the Lord, are being transformed into his very image from glory to glory, as through the Spirit of the Lord" (II Cor. 3:18). We may therefore rely upon the operation of the Holy Ghost in us; He works upon our soul in His silent, ceaseless manner, finally transfiguring and glorifying our soul, and, through it, our body also.

Accordingly, the Holy Spirit *dwells* in the soul of the creature incorporated in Christ. This inhabitation has as its result the sanctifying efficacy of the Holy Spirit in our soul, which is directly manifest in our deification. The soul takes on a resemblance to God, just as the iron held in the fire begins to glow. God "has granted us the very great and precious promises, so that through them you may become partakers of the divine nature" (II Pet. 1:4). This Godlike state of the soul is described by the theological expression *"sanctifying grace."* This is nothing less than a participation in the nature of God, by which we become like unto Him. From this sanctifying grace in the substance of the soul, there results an elevation of all our spiritual faculties; making them Godlike, so that we are empowered to think with and as God thinks, to will and do as He wills and does. In this way we are drawn into the life of the Holy Trinity. God lives in us and the entire Holy Trinity dwells in us as in a holy temple and abides in communion with us. "If anyone love me, he will keep my word, and my Father will love him, and we will come to him and make our abode with him" (John 14:23). A soul adorned with sanctifying grace is, therefore, in spiritual contact with, and participates in, the life of the three divine Persons. The indwelling of the Trinity within us is a consequence of our possession of sanctifying grace; its possession flows from our anointing with the Holy Spirit, who overshadows, or rather floods with light, the creature incorporated in Christ.

Besides sanctifying grace we speak also of *actual grace*, which is a transient help, a stimulation, an enlightenment from God for individual acts. While sanctifying grace denotes a state of soul (its likeness to God), actual grace is a momentary activity of God within the soul. It may precede

a human act, *"prevenient* (preventing, antecedent) grace";
it may coincide with a human act, *"assisting* grace." A special
kind of assisting grace is that of "perseverance," by which
God grants us the privilege of dying in the state of grace.

Grace is absolutely necessary for salvation. Sanctifying
grace is the higher life of the soul and without it the soul is
spiritually dead. Actual grace is given to man for every work
in any way conducive to the supernatural life. By means of
prevenient grace man prepares himself for justification
through sanctifying grace; thus even the very beginning of
salvation is attributable to God.[4] Grace, however, does not
compel man; he can and must cooperate with it, but he is
able to resist it. The cooperation of grace and human liberty
is an inscrutable mystery, because it is the working of God in
man. But one thing is certain: Our freedom is best guarded
and preserved in the hands of Him who created it. "Where
the Spirit of the Lord is, there is freedom" (II Cor. 3:17).
The Church teaches that God gives sufficient grace to all in-
fidels in order that they may believe, and to all sinners that
they may be converted.

Once man has been justified through sanctifying grace, he
will, with the assistance of actual grace, do *good works.* "We
are created in Christ Jesus in good works, which God has
made ready beforehand that we may walk in them" (Eph.
2:10). Good works result naturally from the new state in
which man has been placed by sanctifying grace. It is self-
evident that man must prove by deeds the love that he bears
in his heart for God; otherwise, it would not be genuine
love. Out of this higher life man must bring forth fruits.

---

[4] The necessity of this grace was denied by Pelagius (d. 400) and defended
by St. Augustine (d. 430). The so-called "semi-Pelagians," who were condemned in the year 529, taught that the beginning of justification is from
man.

Since, as our faith teaches, man by justification through Christ becomes intrinsically better, everything he does likewise becomes better. The intrinsic nobility of the soul certainly will reveal itself in one's correspondingly noble conduct. The works we do as branches of the vine (Christ) and as children of God through sanctifying grace are regarded by God as those of His Son and will be accepted by Him with reciprocal love. In other words: Good works performed by us in the state of sanctifying grace are rewarded by God with love in return. Mutual love implies a reciprocal give and take. Accordingly good works earn for us an increase of sanctifying grace and eventually life everlasting. Works done without the state of grace, i.e., not by a child of God and member of Christ, are valueless before God and, so far as eternal salvation is concerned, they are futile. This is the sense in which we are to understand these words of Holy Scripture: "[God] will render to every man according to his works. Life eternal indeed he will give to those who by patience in good works seek glory and honour and immortality" (Rom. 2:6, 7); "Every tree that does not bear good fruit is cut down and thrown into the fire" (Matt. 7:19). The Lord promises eternal life to those who gave Him to eat when He was hungry, to drink when He was thirsty, who harbored, dressed, and visited Him in sickness and in prison; and, on the other hand, He promises eternal fire to those who have denied Him these things in the person of their fellow men (Matt. 25:31–46). Divine Charity, the Holy Spirit, dwells in the former, and not in the latter. But "We know that we have passed from death to life, because we love the brethren. He who does not love, abides in death" (I John 3:14).

Over and above the graces already mentioned there is yet another kind of grace which may be called "graces of state," using the word "state" in a wider sense. Following St. Augustine, theologians call such graces *"gratiae gratis datae,"* graces not given for the benefit of the receiver but for the salvation of others. Here, for instance, belong the graces given to a priest for the fruitful administration of his priesthood. No one is ordained a priest for his own sake, but for the sake of the entire community which requires his services. In this class belongs, too, the grace enabling one to be a good preacher, the gift of being helpful and efficient, and many others.[5] They do not make the receiver any better; they only help him (perhaps entirely without any merit on his part; hence the name *gratis datae*, given as a free gift) to contribute to the welfare of the community. They are for him an incentive not to exalt but to humble himself.

The Holy Spirit, who is imprinted upon our soul, pours out the fullness of *virtues* upon it. By means of the three divine (theological, because their object is God Himself) virtues of Faith, Hope, and Charity, He unites the soul firmly with God in all its thinking, willing, and striving, and directs these faculties toward Him. The four cardinal[6] virtues, Prudence, Justice, Fortitude, and Temperance, guide or set man in proper order in all his relations with himself and others. These virtues are generally inculcated in man by the Holy Spirit but for their effectiveness they require man's zealous cooperation. Their more detailed treatment, however, lies within the province of moral theology.

The Holy Spirit moreover bestows on the soul the so-called *"Seven Gifts."* Following the prophet Isaias, who predicates them of the coming Messias, we may enumerate

---

[5] These functional graces are not limited to any class or group. Every Christian receives such graces.

[6] From the Latin *cardo* — hinge.

them as follows: "the spirit of wisdom, and of understanding, the spirit of counsel, and of fortitude, the spirit of knowledge, and of godliness, and . . . the spirit of the fear of the Lord" (Isa. 11:2). These prompt and qualify man to be attentive to the divine inspirations required to attain his eternal goal and to follow God's guidance, particularly in trials and times of difficulty.

All this splendid wealth bestowed by the Holy Ghost upon everyone united to the Incarnate Son of God is lost by even one mortal sin. A *sin* is a transgression of the divine law, of a commandment of God. Since God does not command capriciously, every sin is contrary to the right order of things precisely because it contradicts reality. Thus, for instance, a lie is contrary to the purpose of human language because God gave language to man that he might be able to express his innermost thoughts. The spoken word is substantially the expression of an internal thought. He that misuses this gift and says something not expressing his thought sins against the essence of human language, and consequently sins against the Creator who necessarily punishes him. Now, since all things are images of God, issuing from His wisdom and formed after His nature, every sin is clearly contrary to the essence of God and to the wisdom flowing from that essence. The Creator watches over His creatures and does not permit them to mar or pervert any being with impunity.

As is well known, we distinguish between mortal sins and venial sins. Mortal sin is so called because it is to the soul what death is to the body: it destroys charity, the source of the higher life. By destroying charity it destroys the quality of adoptive sonship; it undoes the higher, true life of the soul which consists in resemblance to God through sanctifying grace. For this reason, those sins are the greatest which offend directly against God, e.g., infidelity and blasphemy. They disrupt the proper relationship between Creator and creature at the very root. We must always bear in mind that the nature of mortal sin consists in this, that it destroys charity.

To constitute a mortal sin three conditions are necessary: a grave matter, clear knowledge (awareness) of the evil, and full consent of the will. Mortal sin, as has been mentioned, destroys the higher, the true life of the soul which consists in likeness to God through sanctifying grace. The Holy Spirit departs from the soul; it is abandoned by God. The virtues are likewise destroyed.[7] At the same time every possibility of doing anything meritorious or profitable for eternal life is removed; in fact, all merits hitherto acquired are forfeited for eternity.[8] This does not mean that such a man could no longer perform any good work. As a matter of fact he can. The good that he may still do really profits him, for it may move God to grant him the grace of conversion. Under certain circumstances God may grant him temporal rewards or avert temporal punishments. But since such an act does not spring from love of God, God cannot be fully pleased with it, nor can He reward it with eternal happiness. Such an act is worthless in respect to eternity.

Any transgression of the divine law, in which one of the above three conditions is lacking, is a *venial* sin. It is so called because it may be remitted without recourse to the sacrament of penance. A venial sin does not destroy the supernatural life of the soul, nor its union with God. And

[7] The virtues of Faith and Hope remain, unless the sins in question were specifically against these virtues. But they remain in an imperfect state because charity is absent.

[8] These merits, as well as the virtues, are revivified through sincere repentance.

since the love of God is not extinguished, such a soul can always make full reparation by contrition. But conscious and deliberate venial sin, freely and deliberately committed, bears in itself a real peril.

One who seriously strives for perfection will always endeavor to grow in supernatural life and to draw closer to God. In other words, he will desire and seek an ever increasing inflow of divine grace.

CHAPTER VII

THE HOLY AND SANCTIFYING COMMUNITY: THE CHURCH

A MOST conspicuous quality of God's relation with man is its unfailing *social* character. In the beginning He made the first man progenitor of the entire human race, and gave him original justice not so much as a personal gift but as a gift to human nature. So, when Adam fell into sin, he drew the entire race with him into the abyss, and his sin became the sin of the entire race. Christ, too, is a progenitor, a new father of a new race, community, or society, of which He is the head. This society is the Church. Properly speaking, Christ Himself is the Church, and the Church is Christ dwelling among us. The foundation of the Church was laid when Christ died on the cross, for by His death sin, the obstacle to the bestowal of grace upon man, was removed. The day of Pentecost really marks the birthday of the Church, since on that day the Holy Spirit was first diffused over its members, creating and shaping thereby the unity of the Church.

St. Paul styles the Church the *Body* of Christ. The doctrine of this *mystical* Body of Christ is set forth in his Epistles to the Ephesians and to the Colossians. Some of the more striking passages we now quote: "Rather are we to practise the truth in love and so grow up in all things in him who is

the head, Christ. For from him the whole body [being closely
joined and knit together through every joint of the system
according to the functioning in due measure of each single
part] derives its increase to the building up of itself in love"
(Eph. 4:15, 16). "And he [Christ] is before all creatures, and
in him all things hold together. Again, he is the head of his
body, the Church; he, who is the beginning, the firstborn
from the dead, that in all things he may have the first place.
For it has pleased God the Father that in him all his fullness
should dwell, and that through him he should reconcile to
himself all things whether on the earth or in the heavens,
making peace through the blood of his cross" (Col. 1:17–20).
"For in him dwells all the fullness of the Godhead bodily,
and in him who is the head of every Principality and Power
you have received of that fullness" (Col. 2:9, 10). "And may
the peace of Christ reign in your hearts; unto that peace,
indeed, you were called in one body" (Col. 3:15).[1]

The truth which St. Paul expounds by the figure of a
body, with Christ as the head and us as the members, is
fundamentally the same truth as that presented by Christ
Himself under the figure of the vine and its branches. There
is, however, one difference (apart from the fact that the head
is also the seat of spiritual direction); the branches of a vine
are essentially similar, the members of a body dissimilar.
Each of the figures, therefore, stresses in a special way one
aspect of the truth to be expounded. The figure of the vine
exemplifies the immediate relation between each individual
and Christ which is equal for every one. The degree of inti-
macy with Christ depends — after grace — solely upon the will
of the individual, not on the function he has to fulfill in the

[1] The Church is also known as the "Bride of Christ," because she is the
sum total of those persons who are joined to Christ with conscious intent.

Church. The more he opens his soul to admit the life stream issuing from Christ, the more will it actually flow into him, uniting him more and more closely with Christ. In this respect, as this figure of speech teaches, all the members of the Church are equal.

The figure of the body, however, emphasizes not only the connection of each member with the Head, but, above all the variety of functions every member has to perform in the community. This truth is the specific theme elaborated by St. Paul in the twelfth chapter of his First Epistle to the Corinthians (cf. Rom. 12). He speaks there in particular of the wonderful gifts of grace (charisms) found in the primitive Church, and he instructs the faithful endowed with these gifts to employ them for the benefit of others. These gifts are given the faithful not so much for their own use as for that of the community; if they dispense them faithfully, such service also will redound to their salvation. St. Paul speaks as follows: "Now there are varieties of gifts, but the same Spirit; and there are varieties of ministries, but the same Lord; and there are varieties of workings, but the same God, who works all things in all. Now the manifestation of the Spirit is given to everyone for profit. To one through the Spirit is given the utterance of wisdom; and to another the utterance of knowledge, according to the same Spirit; to another faith, in the same Spirit; to another the gift of healing, in the one Spirit; to another the working of miracles; to another prophecy; to another the distinguishing of spirits; to another various kinds of tongues; to another interpretation of tongues. But all these things are the work of one and the same Spirit, who divides to everyone according as he will. For as the body is one and has many members, and all the members of the body, many as they are, form one body, so also is it with Christ. For in one Spirit we were all baptized into one body, whether Jews or Gentiles, whether slaves or free: and we were all given to drink of one Spirit. For the body is not one member, but many. If the foot says, 'Because I am not a hand, I am not of the body,' is it therefore not of the body? And if the ear says, 'Because I am not an eye, I am not of the body': is it therefore not of the body? If the whole body were the eye, where would be the hearing? If the whole body were hearing, where would be the smelling? But as it is, God has set the members, each of them, in the body as he willed. Now if they were all one member, where would the body be? But as it is, there are indeed many members, yet but one body. And the eye cannot say to the hand: 'I do not need thy help'; nor again the head to the feet, 'I have no need of you.' Nay, much rather, those that seem the more feeble members of the body are more necessary. . . . God has so tempered the body together in due portion as to give more abundant honor where it was lacking; that there might be no disunion in the body, but that the members might have care for one another. And if one member suffers anything, all the members suffer with it, or if one member glories, all the members rejoice with it. Now you are the body of Christ, member for member" (I Cor. 12:4–27).

From the text quoted we gather the following conclusions: Christ and the Church constitute one mysterious, but nonetheless real, organism, of which Christ is the Head, i.e., the first and most important member. But since every comparison fits only the truth which it is intended to clarify, we must observe the implied limitations and differences. It is important to note that the head of a natural body cannot exist without, or before, its body, but that Christ exists independently of the Church and existed before her.[2] He contains within Himself the plenitude of grace which God intends to bestow upon the human race. Christ in the course of time unites succeeding generations of men into members of His body and shares with them the fullness of His perfection: "for in him dwells all the fullness of the Godhead bodily, and in him who is the head of every Principality and Power you have received of that fullness" (Col. 2:9, 10).[3] The soul of this body is the Holy Spirit. He lives immediately in Christ, the head, whence He is diffused to the members. He is the life principle of each individual and of the entire community, very much as the human soul provides for the entire body and imparts life to every member of it. He pours forth grace into each member, assigns to it its place in the community, and makes it capable of performing its function and thereby becoming a living part of the vine.

Two considerations must be kept clearly distinct: there is equality of personal worth among the members in so far as they are united with Christ (according to each one's will); there are at the same time differences in the functions of the members. As regards the latter, the intrinsic worth of each member will not be determined by his specific function, but rather by how well he fulfills the place assigned to him by God. In this connection St. Paul makes the noteworthy observation that "God has so tempered the body . . . as to give more abundant honor where it was lacking" (I Cor. 12:24). Just as in the human body the hidden inner organs are of the greatest importance for life, so perhaps he who

[2] The analogy of the vine and the branches is more appropriate here. We must remember to supplement one analogy by the other.

[3] By "principality" and "power" the angels are understood. Christ is also the head of the angels, but not in the same sense that He is the head of men whose nature He assumed.

functions in a relatively hidden manner but endeavors to remain a sound member of Christ may in reality be the most powerful support of the Church. Each member answers for the other, just as all members have a joint responsibility: "If one member suffers anything, all the members suffer with it, or if one member glories, all the members rejoice with it" (I Cor. 12:26). This truth is also the source of the juridical constitution of the Church. She is an organism, in which the members have to work conjointly for the benefit of the community. Therefore she needs a constitution, a hierarchical structure, and necessarily claims the right and the power of proceeding with spiritual punishment against those who behave in a manner harmful to the community. Right and power in the Church are not derived from men, but from Christ. Christ has given to the Church the mission which He received from the Father.

It is to be remembered that not only individuals but also all nations are called to the Church. Racial and individual characteristics have developed in the course of time under the eyes of Divine Providence. To nations as well as individuals were given both a mission and a function for the kingdom of God. The fulfillment of these is the fulfillment of the destiny of the people.

In the thirteenth chapter of his first Epistle to the Corinthians, which follows immediately the chapter in which St. Paul describes the mystical body of Christ, he chants the canticle of love: "If I should speak with the tongues of men and of angels, but do not have charity, I have become as sounding brass, or a tinkling cymbal. And if I have prophecy and know all mysteries and all knowledge, and if I have all faith so as to remove mountains, yet do not have charity, I am nothing. . . . So there abide faith, hope, and charity,

these three; but the greatest of these is charity" (I Cor. 13:1–
3, 13). Love is founded in the common possession of the one
Saviour and forms the entire organism into a wonderful
unity.

The Church is therefore the continuation of Christ in
time. It is the aggregate of individual souls united in Christ:
it is a supernatural organism, a perfect supernatural community. The saints in heaven (Church Triumphant), the
faithful on earth (Church Militant), and the souls in purgatory (Church Suffering) constitute this society. All share
mutually in the spiritual goods of the Church, and all are
mutually helpful to one another. The saints intercede for
us and we may invoke them; we may pray for the Poor
Souls. This is the doctrine of the "Communion of Saints."

From the foregoing we conclude that the Church has the
following marks. She is *one,* for she is the living perpetua-
tion of Christ on earth and constitutes together with Him
the unity of an organism, which unity also appears externally. She is *holy,* for she is Christ Himself; her substance is
holiness, and her purpose is the sanctification of man.[4] She
is *catholic* or universal, because she is destined for all men
and all times; she is Christ living forever, and is the one
means of salvation unto the end of time. Finally, she is
apostolic, since she was founded on the Apostles and formed
in them by the Holy Spirit. Through the Apostles, as
divinely appointed ministers, she has come down to our day
without interruption in her life or mission.

Since the Church is the living Christ on earth, membership in the Church implies membership in Christ. Our personal sanctification depends altogether upon our growth into

[4] This does not contradict the fact that the Church Militant numbers both
good and bad among its members (cf. Matt. 13:24–30, 47–50).

the communal holiness of the Church. There can be nothing more important for us than to live in a most intimate union with that visible Church as quickened and organized by the Holy Spirit. The Church is our "Mother" and the basis of our life; by Her alone can we be saved. This, of course, scarcely implies that a person in good faith outside the Church cannot be saved. Such a one quite properly belongs to the Church; he is already on the way toward her, but is hindered by some insurmountable obstacle. In the eyes of God, who considers here the will rather than the deed, he belongs to the Church. On behalf of the true Church and through her, God grants such a one the graces necessary for salvation. Even in this case, then, the Church is the sole means of salvation. Of course, we must acknowledge that the faithful use of the sacraments in the true Church of Christ pours richer streams of grace upon all who belong entirely to her.

The Church is the living Christ; she carries on His mission of glorifying God and of saving souls. This she does first and foremost by the celebration of the liturgy. The liturgy is the worship that she, as Christ's Mystical Body, celebrates in union with her Head by His command and in His name, as the continuous re-presentation and realization of the mystery of the Redemption. The core and center of this liturgy is the Sacrifice of the Mass. Daily the Church renews Christ's sacrifice on her altars; and daily also she offers her own sufferings united to the sacrifice of Christ. Out of this sacramental offering flow the other sacraments through which the Church sanctifies man.

Finally, the Church continues Christ's work by teaching and by governing; in fine, she faithfully administers the threefold office of Priest, Shepherd, and Teacher entrusted to her by Christ. Because she is, so to speak, Christ continued in the world, His fate is hers: ". . . If they have persecuted me, they will persecute you also; if they have kept my word, they will keep yours also. But all these things they will do to you for my name's sake, because they do not know him who sent me. Because you are not of the world, but I have chosen you out of the world, therefore the world hates you. If the world hates you, know that it has hated me before you. Yes, the hour is coming for everyone who kills you to think that he is offering worship to God. And these things they will do because they have not known the Father nor me" (John 15:20, 21, 19, 18; 16:2, 3). For this reason resurrection and glorification shall likewise be the final lot of the Church.

CHAPTER VIII

THE SACRAMENTS

1. THE SACRAMENTS IN GENERAL

CHRIST has placed Himself at the disposal of the Church and constituted her the dispenser of salvation. This latter fact is especially true of the sacraments where Christ continues His life among the faithful in the transmission of graces to them. Hence the sacraments are called the means of grace. A *sacrament* is an outward sign instituted by Christ through which His grace is conferred upon us. From its very beginning the Church has maintained that Christ instituted seven sacraments: Baptism, Confirmation, Holy Eucharist, Penance, Holy Orders, Matrimony, and Extreme Unction. All the sacraments have these three elements in common: an outward sign, institution by Christ, and interior production of grace.

If we carefully consider the outward sign, we shall see it consists of two parts: *matter* and *form*. The rites and ceremonies and the material used constitute the matter. The words with which the materials are applied and the rites and ceremonies are performed constitute the form. To illustrate: one of the essentials of baptism is the washing with *water* (matter). Its purpose is clearly indicated by the minister when he says: "I baptize thee in the name of the Father and

of the Son and of the Holy Ghost" (form). In this specification of the outward sign, St. Thomas Aquinas sees an intima-
tion of Christ who is the "Word of God," externally
manifested.

By means, then, of this external sign every sacrament becomes a *symbol*. By a symbol we mean a visible representation of the spiritual, of the invisible inner content. In the
sacraments we have a visible representation of some spiritual,
mysterious action, in baptism, for example, of an interior
spiritual cleansing.

A sacrament, however, is no ordinary symbol, but one
given us by Christ, who is God and the Creator Himself. In
devising or depicting a religious symbol, we express a spiritual truth, but we cannot actually unite that symbol with
the truth; when a human artist paints a symbol of God on a
wall, God Himself does not thereby become present. But a
sacrament is a symbol having God for its author, who can
obviously by His almighty power unite the symbol with the
truth symbolized. It is a symbol really containing what it expresses; it is a symbol charged with reality. Accordingly it
not only *symbolizes* spiritual reality but *contains* it. Therefore, St. Thomas defines a sacrament as a sign that causes
what it signifies; it is, in a word, an effective sign. Baptism
not only *signifies* cleansing, but *effects* it.

This last mentioned characteristic of a sacrament emphasizes two things. First, a sacrament is adapted to the nature
of man. Man is a creature, in part spiritual, in part corporeal. All his actions consequently bear the stamp both of
spirit and of matter. His thought is clad in sensible forms
through images and words; his sentiments, to be true and
genuine, must find material expression; spiritual cognitions
are supplied to him through the medium of the senses. This

essential characteristic pervades the entire life of man and all his actions. God, too, has adapted Himself to this characteristic; He has joined His graces with certain outward signs in which the internal efficacy is embodied. In this manner the body is sanctified and partakes of the supernatural.

In the second place, we can consider the sacraments as radiations of the Incarnation. Just as in the Incarnation the invisible Son of God became visible and took a body in order to move among men as one of them, so, too, His presence in the sacrament is, as it were, a continuous Incarnation. Pope St. Leo I says very beautifully: "That which was visible in our Saviour passed over into the sacraments" (Sermon 74). According to St. Thomas Aquinas, Christ is the Sacrament of sacraments, and all the other sacraments are radiations of this original sacrament.

Considered in this light, the sacraments are continuations of Christ's activity. Christ is the real minister of the sacraments, as He is also their author. As God, He is the first cause of the grace produced by the sacraments. As man, He is the instrumental cause, for it is through the instrumentality of His humanity that Christ effects our salvation. In every sacrament then, the divinity *and* humanity of the God-Man are active. In fact, as St. Thomas Aquinas explicitly states, there is in the sacraments a coactivity of the God-Man and His redemptive work. Christ's suffering and resurrection are, so to speak, imparted to us through the sacraments. The actions of Christ are an instrument of our salvation in the hands of God: "The suffering and resurrection attain efficacy by spiritual contact with us in faith and in the sacraments" (cf. *Summa Theologica,* III, q. 48, a. 6; q. 56, a. 1 and 2). Through the sacraments we come into contact with Christ, or in particular, with His suffering and resurrection. By this

means, the "graceful" efficacy of the redemptive work flows
to us; the Redemption is given to us, and each and every one
of us is redeemed.

The human minister of the sacraments (e.g., a priest) is an
instrument in the hands of Christ. But since Christ is the
true and final minister of the sacraments, the effect of a
sacrament will not depend upon the disposition of the
human minister. Even though he were in the state of mortal
sin, and did not himself believe in its efficacy, the sacrament
would be valid and would produce its effect, provided that
he administer it according to the intention of the Church.
This efficacy, independent of the disposition of the minister,
is styled in the Latin language *ex opere operato,* "in virtue
of the action performed." From this efficacy *ex opere operato*
it follows that the effect of the sacrament will enter into the
soul more deeply than any human operation. One man can
act upon another only extrinsically. He may train him to
the extent that he will elicit certain reactions, he may draw
out that which is at the root of his being, but he cannot
effect a change in the very core of man's being, he cannot
improve the will of a man determined to remain bad. In this
respect he is powerless and has reached the limit of his influence. God, however, who works upon us in the sacraments,
operates in the depths of our being. He works upon its very
core and makes it better; he gives us an entirely new Godlike *being.* Because the sacrament confers on us a higher
kind of being, it improves the will causing it to desire the
good previously neglected, and to desire and strive for it
more energetically than ever before.[1]

---

[1] We should, therefore, put our entire trust in the efficacy of the sacraments. Even though their reception produces no sensible reaction, we know
that they operate on the very essence of our being, and will become fruitful
for our spiritual life.

The sacraments, as is now evident, are the works of God and not of man. Therefore their efficacy is really not dependent upon the one who receives them. Naturally, a person must have the intention to receive the sacrament, otherwise it would not be conferred. Moreover he must desire the grace of the sacrament, otherwise he would receive it unworthily and the graces would not become effective.

Since the sacraments were instituted by Christ, the Church can change nothing that belongs to their essence. Christ has entrusted them to the Church to be administered by her; she may and must make rules for their worthy administration.[2]

If we consider the efficacy of the individual sacraments, we see first of all that they bring us into contact with the God-Man and His redemptive work. Every sacrament effects incorporation in the sonship of God, and an infusion or increase of sanctifying grace. A sacrament instituted primarily for the infusion of sanctifying grace is called a sacrament of the dead. The others (since they presuppose the presence of sanctifying grace) increase it and are called sacraments of the living. Apart from sanctifying grace every sacrament produces "sacramental grace," i.e., a claim to the actual graces necessary for a life corresponding to the nature of the respective sacrament. For example, parties contracting marriage receive, besides sanctifying grace, a claim throughout life upon all actual graces needed to live as Christian husband and wife. Every sacrament has its own unique character and its efficacy moves with certain set limits, as one can gather from the outward sign of the sacrament.

[2] When the Church places certain conditions for the valid reception of the sacraments of Penance and Marriage, she does not intend to modify the essence of these sacraments.

Several of the sacraments also impress an indelible mark (character) upon the soul. These are the sacraments which impart a special consecration to man: Baptism, Confirmation, and Holy Orders. This indelible mark, or sacramental character, implies participation in Christ's priesthood. Baptism confers a general priesthood; Confirmation develops this character; and Holy Orders confers the official priesthood. If any one of these three sacraments, as well as Matrimony and Extreme Unction (generally not received a second time) is received unworthily, i.e., with defective disposition on the part of the one receiving them, it is nevertheless validly conferred, although its grace will become operative only when the proper disposition is present.

Here we must touch upon an important question. It was stated that faith has power to bring us into contact with Christ. We quoted St. Paul to the effect: "That he [the Father] may grant you from his glorious riches . . . to have Christ dwelling through faith in your hearts" (Eph. 3:16–17). In a certain sense, the same efficacy is attributed to faith as to sacraments worthily received. This is also the teaching of Holy Scripture, especially in regard to the two most necessary sacraments: baptism and the Holy Eucharist. For instance, St. Paul, writing to the Galatians, speaks almost indiscriminately of faith in Christ and baptism in Christ: "For you are all the children of God through faith in Christ Jesus. For all you who have been baptized into Christ, have put on Christ" (Gal. 3:26, 27). The Lord Himself makes a similar and scarcely perceptible transition in regard to the Eucharist, when in the synagogue at Capharnaum He promised this sacrament (John 6:32–71). He speaks at first in general terms of men coming to Him and believing in Him. In the second part, however, these generalities point more and more to the reception of His flesh and blood after the manner of earthly food.

From these testimonies we may infer that faith is perfected in the reception of the sacraments. As has been said, man is a being composed of spirit and matter; all his actions bear the stamp of spirituality and corporeality. His internal spiritual acts (exercise of intellect and will) are, therefore, completed only when they have been manifested externally, and have taken body, as it were. Only in this way can they have a social value. Purely internal acts are negligible so far as the outside world is concerned. Internal act and external act constitute a unity which may be compared to that of the soul and body. So, faith in Christ is not complete before God, unless it has taken body — has assumed outward expression in the reception of the sacrament. Internal faith and external reception of a sacrament (especially of baptism and the Eucharist) constitute a unity and belong together like soul and body.[3] St. Thomas Aquinas speaks of sacraments as "sacraments of faith," and especially of baptism which he calls "*the* sacrament of faith." Only by the outward reception of a sacrament is our internal faith made perfect and serviceable for the community, just as internal faith in its turn animates the reception of the sacrament.[4]

Closely bound up with the notion of sacrament is the notion of sacramental. The sacramentals are so called because they bear some resemblance to the sacraments. They differ from the latter in this — that they were not instituted

[3] From what has been said, we can more readily grasp that God can accept the will to do a deed in place of the deed itself in the case of a person who, through inculpable ignorance or some external obstacle, does not receive the sacraments.

[4] It is hardly necessary to point out, however, that the sacraments are not a mere expression of our faith. They are an expression and sign of our faith, but much more than that.

by Jesus Christ but by the Church. To this class belong numerous blessings of the Church — blessed objects and their use, holy water, palms, candles, etc. Their efficacy is not infallible nor as thorough as that of the sacraments. They do not produce their effect *ex opere operato* but *ex opere operantis,* i.e., in virtue of the one performing the action. Their efficacy depends, first of all, on the intercessory power of the Church, and for that reason their effectiveness very closely approaches that of the sacraments. This holds true especially of many blessings, as, e.g., the consecration of churches. Secondarily, the efficacy of the sacramentals depends on the devotion of the faithful using them. Sacramentals do not of themselves produce sanctifying grace, although the one using them devotedly may receive an increase of grace, but they do secure special protection and help from God through the prayers of the Church. Their chief importance lies in this — that they dedicate objects of everyday use to the service of God and make them profitable for the children of God. By means of the sacramentals the Church dedicates all nature to Christ. Of special value are the benedictions or consecrations that withdraw an object from secular use and place it in the service of God; such would be the dedication of churches, the blessing of sacred vessels and vestments. Even though the use of sacramentals is not of obligation for the faithful, they should treat with due reverence things that the Church has blessed. But they should not put them to superstitious use, i.e., seek from a person or thing an efficacy that neither by nature nor by the will of God is given it.

2. BAPTISM AND CONFIRMATION

The first and most necessary of the sacraments is baptism. Its outward sign consists in the pouring of water upon the head of the one to be baptized while saying: "I baptize thee in the name of the Father and of the Son and of the Holy Ghost." Anyone may validly baptize, and in cases of necessity natural water suffices. Solemn baptism with its attendant ceremonies is the function of the parish priest, who may authorize another priest or a deacon. Ordinarily, the priest uses "baptismal water," which has been specially blessed on Holy Saturday and on the Vigil of Pentecost. Solemn baptism is administered with a number of attendant ceremonies. In the early ages of Christianity it was customary to baptize on Holy Saturday or on the Vigil of Pentecost. According to present custom, baptism may be administered on any day; but the Church desires the baptism of adults to take place on Holy Saturday. Christ instituted the sacrament when, after the Resurrection and shortly before the Ascension, He said to His disciples: "All power in heaven and on earth has been given to me. Go, therefore, and make disciples of all nations, baptizing them in the name of the Father, and of the Son, and of the Holy Spirit teaching them to observe all that I have commanded you; and behold, I am with you all days, even unto the consummation of the world" (Matt. 28:18–20).

The essence of baptism has been briefly indicated in previous pages. That baptism is a rebirth from water and the Holy Spirit is evident from the words of Christ to Nicodemus. Baptism is incorporation in Christ, the first and fundamental contact with Him. In His Epistle to the Romans St. Paul gives us a profound instruction on and clear insight into baptism: "Do you not know that all we who have been baptized into Christ Jesus have been baptized into his death? For we were buried with him by means of baptism into death, in order that, just as Christ has arisen from the dead through the glory of the Father, so we also may walk in newness of life. For if we have been united with him in the likeness of his death, we shall be so in the likeness of his resurrection also. . . . If we have died with Christ, we believe that we shall also live together with Christ" (Rom. 6:3–8).

According to St. Paul we are baptized — immersed[5] — *into* Christ. But baptism, the Apostle tells us, is not only an immersion into Christ, but also into the death of Christ. Baptism, then, is a union with, an identification with the redemptive death of Christ. By it we are incorporated in His redemptive work and thereby partake actively in the work of redemption. We are redeemed internally; with Christ and *in* Him, i.e., by union with Him, we have made satisfaction for our sins. Hence Christ's merits have not been simply imputed to us extrinsically, but they have entered into us, have penetrated our being, and have become ours. We have in some mysterious way hung upon the cross with Christ. Thus have we participated in His redemptive work; thus have we been identified with it. This means that we ourselves, being subject to the death sentence due us for sin, have had it executed upon us, so that we have been immolated in and with Christ Himself. So it comes about that in and with Christ this sentence is nullified and indeed obliterated. Our death in the body is anticipated and by its alliance with the death of Christ loses its sting, its power to harm.

After baptism our life keeps pace with that of Christ. His life and ours flow in the same channel so that Christ relives His redemptive life in us and we in turn renew His in us.

[5] The original meaning of the Greek and Latin term for "baptize" was "immerse." This would doubtless indicate that in the early Christian era baptism was administered by immersion. But, as St. Paul indicates in the text quoted above, the term has a deeper significance.

St. Paul, in his several Epistles, presents this life made one with Christ in words admirably suited to express its wonderful truth. He teaches that the Christian suffers with Christ, is crucified with Him, dies with Him, and is buried with Him. The Christian rises with Christ, is quickened with Him, and is glorified together with Him. God has transported the Christian together with Christ into heaven, where he reigns with Him as His coheir. St. Paul expresses the same truth in the following general terms: the Christian resembles Christ; he is implanted in Him, engrafted upon Him, has a share in Him, forms one body with Him (as all Christians are in turn one body), and is united with Him. The briefest formula of all is the phrase used a hundred and sixty-four times throughout Paul's Epistles: "In Christ Jesus." Every baptized person may truly say of himself, as did St. Paul: "With Christ I am nailed to the cross. It is now no longer I that live, but Christ lives in me" (Gal. 2:19, 20). That is why the Fathers referred to a Christian as another Christ; and why St. Ignatius of Antioch, Martyr, calls himself and the faithful "Christ bearers."

The nature of baptism determines its particular *effects*. First of all, it destroys original sin, and this is really its essential effect. In this way comes about the spiritual rebirth in Christ, a birth that corresponds to carnal generation from Adam. But baptism also remits all the personal sins committed by the individual before baptism, and moreover all the punishments due to sin. It infuses into the soul sanctifying grace and all the virtues mentioned above. While many effects of original sin — concupiscence especially — remain in us after baptism, they have lost their sinful character, the taint of culpability, and now become instruments for our purification. To sum up, baptism is incorporation in Christ and is consequently incorporation in the Church, the living extension of Christ on earth.

Another effect of baptism (which will be better understood when we speak of the Holy Eucharist) is that it impresses upon our souls the indelible character described above as a participation in the priesthood of Christ. Baptism qualifies man to receive all the other sacraments, i.e., it is a preliminary condition for them. It qualifies him, above all, to celebrate Holy Mass with the priest, to act as a co-offerer of that Sacrifice which is the re-presentation of the sacrifice of the cross. St. Peter calls the baptized a "holy priesthood," a "royal priesthood" (I Pet. 2:5, 9). This general, or universal priesthood is conferred by baptism; the sacramental character unites forever the Christian with Christ, the High Priest. The Christian remains extrinsically united to Christ, even though he be in the state of mortal sin. By sin the Christian cuts himself off from the fullness of graces that flow from Christ. He becomes a dead member, a withered branch on the vine. Should he remain in this state to the end, he will experience those words of the Lord: "Every branch in me that bears no fruit he will take away; and every branch that bears fruit he will cleanse, that it may bear more fruit. . . . If anyone does not abide in me, he shall be cast outside as the branch and wither; and they shall gather them up, and cast them into the fire and they shall burn" (John 15:2–6). The eventual outcome can only be final reprobation, or exclusion from Christ. But previous to that, he remains throughout in some degree united with Him. He need but reopen his heart to grace and he will again become a living member. Thus it is that conversion after sin is an easier matter for the baptized than for the unbaptized.[6]

---

[6] The sacramental character, on the other hand, implies a responsibility, and for the condemned soul, an increase of punishment.

The necessity of baptism is evident from these words of the Lord: "Go into the whole world and preach the gospel to every creature. He who believes and is baptized shall be saved, but he who does not believe shall be condemned" (Mark 16:15, 16). "Amen, amen, I say to thee, unless a man be born again of water and the Spirit, he cannot enter into the kingdom of God" (John 3:5). Baptism is therefore absolutely necessary.

According to very ancient tradition, martyrdom for the Christian faith is equivalent to baptism of water. A martyr is baptized in his own blood which he sheds for Christ. By his death he is made conformable to Christ who died for him. This is "Baptism of Blood." Furthermore we should recall here what has been said concerning the relation between faith and the sacraments. It is absolutely necessary to be in contact with Christ. This contact is normally effected by an internal act expressed externally in the sacrament. In case an unavoidable external hindrance precludes placing the external act, God can accept the internal act, i.e., the will, for the deed itself. If then, anyone is prepared to do what God requires of him in order to be saved, he will have in the eyes of God received baptism. This is "Baptism of Desire." Although he will be saved, he does not receive the indelible character which baptism of water alone imprints upon the soul. As a consequence, he is excluded from receiving the other sacraments.

It is an ancient practice of the Church to baptize infants. St. Augustine says: "Such has always been the custom in the Church; thus she received it from the faith of the Fathers; thus she will constantly observe it to the end," and he traces the custom of baptizing infants back to Apostolic tradition. In the baptism of infants, the Church, through the sponsors, performs the internal acts which the child is incapable of making.

The sacrament of confirmation (from the Latin *firmare* — to strengthen) develops and strengthens that which baptism has implanted. Just as a man, after he is born, grows by degrees, so, too, in the supernatural life, birth must be followed by increase and development. Confirmation, then, implies the fullness of that which baptism confers. Since the fullness of grace is in a very special manner described as the possession of the Holy Spirit, confirmation truly is the sacrament of the Holy Spirit, in which the recipient receives Him. Confirmation develops the baptismal character in that it calls upon the Christian to cooperate for the common good of the Church. An infant thinks only of his own interests, but in more mature years he will begin to think of others also. The confirmed Christian will begin to feel an obligation toward all the members of God's kingdom.

Now, it is a matter of doctrine that the Holy Spirit is operative in the Church. In the early days of Christianity, when the sacrament of confirmation was administered, the Holy Spirit frequently made miraculous distribution of His gifts, so necessary for the growth of the youthful Church: the gift of tongues, prophecy, etc. The appearance of these gifts testified to the presence of the Holy Spirit. This is described for the first time in the Acts of the Apostles in the following words: "When the Apostles in Jerusalem heard that Samaria had received the word of God, they sent to them Peter and John. On their arrival they prayed for them that they might receive the Holy Spirit; for as yet he had not come upon any of them, but they had only been baptized in the name of the Lord Jesus. Then they laid their hands on them and they received the Holy Spirit" (Acts 8:14–17).

This must have been accompanied by some charismatic phenomena. For "when Simon (the magician) *saw* that the Holy Spirit was given through the laying on of the apostles' hands, he offered them money," because he also wished to acquire these miraculous powers.[7] The same phenomena occurred when St. Paul baptized and confirmed some disciples of John the Baptist at Ephesus. "And when Paul laid his hands on them, the Holy Spirit came upon them, and they began to speak in tongues and to prophesy" (Acts 19:6). If the Holy Spirit does not dispense these wonderful gifts today, He does nevertheless come in the sacrament of confirmation to impart such power to the recipient as will be useful in building up the body of the Church. And so in this sense also, confirmation is the sacrament of the Holy Spirit who is the soul of the Church and abides in her.

Today confirmation is ordinarily administered by the bishop. He lays his hand upon the head of the confirmant, and at the same time anoints his forehead with chrism (made of olive oil mixed with aromatic substances), and says: "I sign thee with the sign of the cross and confirm thee with the chrism of salvation in the name of the Father, and of the Son and of the Holy Ghost. Amen." The pope may also authorize an ordinary priest to administer confirmation.[8]

Confirmation increases sanctifying grace, and impresses an indelible character upon the soul. It confers the Holy Spirit in order to strengthen the receiver and it encourages him to confess his faith fearlessly, and to labor zealously. Confirmation is not absolutely necessary for salvation, but neglecting to receive it through indifference would be sinful.

[7] Whence the word "simony" — selling spiritual values for money.
[8] All the priests of the Eastern Church, in which confirmation is given immediately after baptism, possess this authorization.

3. THE MOST HOLY SACRAMENT OF THE ALTAR

The greatest of the sacraments, on which all the others focus, is the Most Holy Sacrament of the Altar. It is the summit of the Christian life and, in a certain sense, the entire content of Christianity. From earliest Christian times, this sacrament was designated by the term "Eucharist," which literally means "Thanksgiving."[9]

The Eucharist is both a true sacrifice and a true sacrament; it is a sacramental sacrifice and a sacrificial sacrament, in other words, Holy Mass, including Holy Communion. We will, therefore, consider the Eucharist both as Holy Mass (Sacrifice) and as Holy Communion. We shall first discuss the real presence of Christ under the species of bread and wine, then the sacramental presence in the Holy Sacrifice of the Mass, and finally Holy Communion. We must emphasize, however, that this systematic arrangement does not imply actual division in the unity of the eucharistic "Sacrifice-Sacrament."

The real presence of Christ under the species of bread and wine is attested to, first of all, by the words which the Saviour used in promising the Eucharist. The evening previous, He had wrought two great miracles: first, in a solitary spot on the shore of Lake Genesareth, He multiplied the loaves (John 6:1–15); and later the same evening He walked over the waters to His disciples who were struggling to keep their little boat from capsizing (John 6:16–21). The multiplication of the loaves manifested the power Christ had over bread, and the walking on the water the power over His own body. On the following day in the synagogue at Caphar-

[9] The celebration of the Holy Eucharist was accompanied by a solemn service of thanksgiving to God for all His wondrous deeds.

naum, He promised that sacrament which is His body under the form of bread (John 6:22–71): " 'The bread that I will give is my flesh for the life of the world.' The Jews on that account argued with one another, saying: 'How can this man give us His flesh to eat?' [Obviously they had given a literal interpretation to His words.] Jesus therefore said to them: 'Amen, amen, I say to you, unless you eat the flesh of the Son of Man, and drink his blood, you shall not have life in you. He who eats my flesh and drinks my blood has life everlasting and I will raise him up on the last day. For my flesh is food indeed: and my blood is drink indeed. He who eats my flesh and drinks my blood, abides in me and I in him. As the living Father has sent me, and I live because of the Father, so he who eats me, he also shall live because of me.' " The Saviour, you will notice, retracts not one of His words; on the contrary, He confirms them by a solemn oath.

When many of His disciples withdrew from Him because of this "hard saying," He suggested that his twelve apostles go also. But listen to Peter: "Lord, to whom shall we go? Thou hast words of everlasting life, and we have come to believe and to know that thou art the Christ, the Son of God" (John 6:69–70). Only one thing the Redeemer deigns to explain further: "It is the spirit that gives life, the flesh profits nothing," i.e., it is my flesh glorified, spiritualized, filled with the Holy Spirit, which I will give to you as food; this alone is life-giving. "What then if you should see the Son of Man ascending where he was before?" (John 6:63, 64); i.e., my glorification following the Resurrection and Ascension will prove conclusively that the flesh I will give you is "spirit," spiritualized, life-giving.

The Real Presence of Christ is again clearly expressed in the words with which the Saviour instituted the Holy Sacrament at the Last Supper: "Take and eat, this is my Body which shall be given for you. All of you drink of this; for this is my Blood of the new Covenant, which is being shed for many unto the forgiveness of sins. Do this in remembrance of me."

These words have at all times been understood to signify the Real Presence. Faith in the Real Presence of Christ stood an established and acknowledged truth for fully sixteen centuries; even Luther insisted on the Real Presence, although in a somewhat different manner than Catholics ("in and with and under the unchanged bread and only at the moment of reception" — according to Luther).

The manner in which Christ becomes present in the Holy Sacrament is termed "transubstantiation" (from the Latin *substantia,* substance, essence, plus *trans,* across; i.e., transition from one substance to another, transubstantiation, a substantial change). The words of consecration, which the priest, as an ambassador and instrument of Christ, speaks over the bread and wine, change the substance of the bread into the substance of the body of Christ, and likewise change the substance of wine into the substance of the blood of Christ, only the appearances, the sensible forms of bread and wine, remaining.

Logically we distinguish between the outward form of a thing and its essence. The former is perceived by the senses, but the latter is apprehended by the intellect alone. For example, suppose I perceive an object change in all its outward form; yet am I not aware that in certain particulars the object is still the same? Outwardly the seed of grain indeed differs from the full-grown plant, and so, too, does the caterpillar from the butterfly. Notwithstanding these facts, I know that both before and after, the same "thing" somehow remains, i.e., the same essence, the same substance remains, which I cannot perceive by the senses but only by the intellect. Similarly we distinguish between the outward forms of bread and wine, and the "thing itself" or the substance. In the world of nature the outward form and corresponding substance are always in combination; an object *appears* to be just what it is and not something else. But in the consecrated host (Latin *hostia,* sacrificed victim, or sacrificial gift) and in the consecrated wine, the only outward forms present are the species of bread and wine. By divine omnipotence, the Body and Blood of Christ are "hidden" beneath forms properly foreign to them. We are certain of this by divine revelation and the same fact is expressed in the words of consecration. For this reason we do not see the Body and Blood of Christ; we only grasp them with the eyes of faith. In fine, we believe the Saviour and His word.

Under the outward forms of bread and wine, the Body and Blood of Christ remain present just as long as the outward forms themselves are present. He is among us in the same manner as He now is in heaven. So it is that the entire Saviour, body and soul, as God and as man, is present under each species and in every part of that species, even though by the words of the priest the bread is changed into the Lord's Body and the wine into His Blood. Theologians say that although by the words of consecration the Body is present under the form of bread and the Blood under the form of wine, yet in virtue of living unity, the whole living Saviour is present under each form, with flesh and blood, with body and soul, as God and as man. The Body of the Saviour is present in a sublime and spiritualized manner. It is the selfsame body that hung upon the cross, but a Body now transfigured and spiritualized.

What we have been saying clearly shows that we owe adoration and honor to the Most Holy Sacrament of the Altar. We speak of the Sacrament of the *Altar*. Wherever there is an altar, there is sacrifice. The Sacrament of the Altar is therefore a sacrifice: the Holy *Sacrifice of the Mass*.

The Holy Sacrifice of the Mass is the unbloody re-enactment and actual making present of the sacrifice of the cross. This statement expresses the essence of Holy Mass. We have seen that a sacrament is a holy sign that effects what it signifies; it is a symbol which the Creator Himself has charged with reality. To consider the symbolism of the Sacrifice of the Mass, we turn first to the solemn moment of consecration, the climax of Holy Mass. At that sacred moment, the Flesh and Blood of Christ become present under the *separate* forms of bread and wine. The Flesh and Blood of Christ *appear* on our altars as separated from one another, thereby symbolizing the separation of the blood from the body or the shedding of blood. Now, what is actually symbolized is the real shedding of the blood of Christ on the cross ("This is my Body, which is given for you. This is my Blood, which shall be shed for you and for many"). We have previously noted that the sacraments are God-given symbols containing the reality they symbolize. Evidently then, this symbolized reality is present and actually contained in them. Therefore, the shedding of the blood of Christ on Golgotha, symbolized in Holy Mass, is really sacramentally present in Holy Mass.[10]

Holy Mass is not "a repetition" of the sacrifice of the cross. That would be contrary to the inspired word of St. Paul in his Epistle to the Hebrews, where he expressly states:

[10] The phrase "sacramentally present" indicates that there is a difference in the mode of presence between the historical sacrifice of Christ and the sacrifice of the Mass, although the latter is no less real than the former.

"Nor yet has he [Christ] entered to offer himself often, as the high priest [of the Old Testament] enters into the Holies year after year with blood not his own [the sacrifices of the Old Testament could not actually redeem]; for in that case he must have suffered often since the beginning of the world. But as it is, once for all at the end of the ages, he has appeared for the destruction of sin by the sacrifice of himself. . . . And every priest [of the Old Testament] indeed stands daily ministering, and often offering the same sacrifices, which can never take away sins; but Jesus, having offered *one* sacrifice for sins, has taken his seat forever at the right hand of God" (Heb. 9:25, 26; 10:11, 12). It would be derogatory to the sacrifice of the cross to say that it is "repeated" in Holy Mass. It is not "repeated" but renewed in an unbloody manner, or, rather, made actually present again sacramentally. Holy Mass is a commemorative sacrifice, instituted by Christ with the words: "Do this in remembrance of me." The Roman Catechism says: "We confess, that it is, and must be held to be one and the same sacrifice which is accomplished at Mass and which was accomplished on the cross; in the same manner as it is one and the same victim, namely, Christ our Lord, who offered Himself only once in a bloody manner on the altar of the cross. For the bloody and the unbloody victim are not two victims but one, the offering of which is re-enacted daily in the Eucharist according to the command of the Lord: 'Do this in remembrance of me.' There is also only one and the same priest, Christ the Lord" (Part I, Chap. 4, 61 f.). Christ Himself is thus victim and priest at Holy Mass. The priest, celebrating the Holy Mass, is but an instrument in His hand.

The Eucharistic Sacrifice is likewise offered at the hands of the Church (through the priest). Thus the full essence and meaning of Holy Mass is manifested. In Holy Mass the *entire* Christ — the head and the members — offers Himself to the Father. Christ desires to offer His sacrifice *for* us and *with* us. Holy Mass makes it possible for all Christians of all countries and times to take part in the holy sacrifice of the cross, the one sacrifice of the New Testament. At Holy Mass Christ offers up His sacrifice with the Church and through the Church. Consequently, Holy Mass is the sacrifice of the Church as well. For this reason the Church contributes her part to the holy sacrifice in gifts of bread and wine. She offers up to the heavenly Father in her own name the sacrifice which Christ offered upon the cross. And indeed the universal Church is always active in every Holy Mass. Every Mass is a public official act, though it be offered without ceremonious pomp and splendor. Strictly speaking, a "private Mass," in the sense of a "private affair" is impossible. The entire Church, and especially the congregation actually present at Mass, together offer the sacrifice with and through the priest. By baptism we received our capacity for cooperation in offering the sacrifice, because baptism is our ordination to the general priesthood. A baptized person taking part in Holy Mass does so not passively but actively and effectively, as a co-offerer. In the Canon of the Mass the priest makes mention of all those present "for whom we offer, or who offer up to Thee this sacrifice of praise." At every Holy Mass then we participate in the redemptive sacrifice of Christ; we render satisfaction with Christ and in Christ, and in consequence are personally redeemed. God sees, as it were, all Christendom standing gathered round the cross of Christ, and offering with mankind's divinely appointed High Priest the one sacrifice of the New Law, the redemptive sacrifice. Christendom joins Christ in accomplishing the highest worship of God, in which every creature fulfills its destiny. We are indeed "a holy priesthood, a royal priesthood" (I Pet. 2:5, 9).[11]

Participation in the sacrifice of Christ and application of the redemption and merits which He acquired on the cross are realized most intimately and abundantly in *Holy Communion*. Holy Communion is the banquet of the sacrifice, the partaking of the Body and Blood of Christ, of the Body sacrificed on the cross and gloriously risen. Holy Communion increases sanctifying grace; weakens evil tendencies; produces a joy and a power for good; cleanses from venial and shields against mortal sin,[12] and gives us life everlasting and a glorious resurrection of the body. The Saviour has assured us: "He who eats my flesh and drinks my blood has life everlasting and I will raise him up on the last day" (John 6:55). The Eucharist was accordingly called by St. Ignatius of Antioch "the medicine of immortality."[13]

From practical, but not dogmatic, motives, the Western Church from the thirteenth century onward has administered Holy Communion only under one kind, that of bread. The Sacred Blood is easily exposed to irreverence in the

[11] Man should make an offering of his own person to God. He should join his sufferings to those of Christ so as to continue Christ's work of redemption. St. Paul wrote from his Roman captivity to the community at Collossae: "I rejoice now in the sufferings I bear for your sake; and what is lacking of the sufferings of Christ I fill up in my flesh for his body, which is the Church" (Col. 1:24).

[12] Holy Communion cleanses from mortal sin when the recipient is at the time unconscious of grievous guilt. Nevertheless, the obligation to confess the sin remains.

[13] The Holy Eucharist is more than the celebration of Christ's passion and death. It is the celebration as well of His resurrection and glorification. His very death is glorified. (On the whole, all the sacraments can be called the effect of the glorification of Christ.) Participation in His death implies participation in His victory and, consequently, in His resurrection and glorification.

distribution of Communion. Because Christ is present entire (Body and Blood, Soul and Divinity) under the species of bread, the faithful are deprived of nothing. Thus they fulfill the command of Christ to eat His flesh and drink His blood when they communicate under one kind only. For sacrifice, however, consecration of both species is necessary. Once this has been accomplished, the partaking of the least particle of the sacrificial offering is a participation in the entire sacrifice.

Holy Communion is the nourishment of the soul. St. Thomas Aquinas says that God has provided for our supernatural life much as He has provided for our natural, temporal life. Birth alone is not sufficient; to maintain life, to grow and develop, the child must be nourished and cared for. We, too, in order to preserve the supernatural life which we received as a free gift in baptism, need nourishment for the soul. This food of our souls is Holy Communion. The necessity of receiving it frequently is evident from the words of Christ: "Amen, amen, I say to you, unless you eat the flesh of the Son of Man, and drink his blood, you shall not have life in you" (John 6:54). In her fifth commandment the Church has ruled that every Catholic who has reached the age of discretion must approach the table of the Lord at least once a year, at Easter time. More frequent reception, however, may, on occasion, become of strict obligation; such would be the case of one exposed to special dangers, and above all, where there is danger of relapse into mortal sin. One thing is certain: Holy Communion will always be a *sine qua non* of spiritual progress.

Because the Holy Eucharist is a food, it is a sacrament of the living. Consequently, for its reception the recipient must be in the state of grace. If the soul is in the state of mortal sin, previous confession is necessary.[14] An unworthy Communion, the reception of the Holy Eucharist by one conscious of mortal sin unremitted by confession, is a sacrilege, the profanation of the Body and Blood of Christ. The Church, moreover, demands the observance of a fast from midnight.[15]

The Holy Eucharist is the summit of the Christian life. By this sacrament we give God the adoration and homage due Him and offer satisfaction for our sins. In it is found redemption and salvation for man. Holy Communion is precisely what its name signifies: a union between God and man and a union of men with one another. The Fathers of the Church embraced this truth and saw an indication of it in the fact that the Eucharist is present under forms which best represent the union of the many in one: out of many grapes the wine, out of many kernels the bread.

4. PENANCE

The sacrament of penance is that sacrament in which the priest, under God, forgives sins committed after baptism. Christ instituted the sacrament on the day of His Resurrection when, appearing to His Apostles in the supper room, He breathed on them and said: "Receive the Holy Spirit;

[14] We can now see the need to prepare ourselves for Holy Communion by exciting the acts of desire for our sacramental Redeemer. The more receptive we are to the grace of God, the greater will our portion be. It is noteworthy that Pius X, the "Pope of the Holy Eucharist," moderated all extravagant demands of preparation for Holy Communion. Holy Communion is a medicine and a communication of life, not a reward. The best preparation, practically speaking, is to take an active part in the celebration of Holy Mass.

[15] In 1906, Pius X relaxed the obligation of fasting for persons confined for a month by sickness, whose speedy recovery is doubtful. On the judgment of their confessor, they may be permitted to receive Holy Communion once or twice a week, notwithstanding that they may have taken medicine or some liquid.

whose sins you shall forgive, they are forgiven them; and whose sins you shall retain, they are retained" (John 20:22, 23). Penance was instituted after the manner of a judicial trial. The judge (priest) is to decide whether the sins of the penitent are to be forgiven or retained. For this judgment he must know them, and the accuser can be none other than the sinner himself.

Hence Penance was established and has always been practiced in the form that the single sins are confessed in detail and not merely in general. An even more cogent reason for this is the fact that only by the external acknowledgment of the sin committed does man, as a corporeal-spiritual being, complete logically his internal conversion, i.e., the negation of the deed committed. Furthermore, in confession made to a priest and in absolution received from him as the representative of the Church, the sinner can find pardon from the community for his sin. In addition to secret or auricular confession the early Church knew and practiced public confession. The latter was sometimes imposed on those who had committed sin publicly. The penance due to sin was usually performed publicly.

The external signs of this sacrament are the acts of the penitent, i.e., his confession and contrition expressed in some external way, together with the words of the priest: "I absolve thee from thy sins in the name of the Father and of the Son and of the Holy Ghost. Amen." Evidently the remission or the retention of sins is not a matter of whim with the priest. He is entirely an instrument in the hand of Christ and must judge as His representative.

All sins committed after baptism can be forgiven in the sacrament of penance. If there is mention in Holy Scripture of sins that cannot be forgiven, what is meant is stubborn impenitence and deliberate rejection of the Saviour by the sinner. All in the state of mortal sin are obliged to receive the sacrament of penance in confession.

The acts requisite for the penitent are in particular: examination of conscience, contrition and purpose of amendment, confession and satisfaction. Examination of conscience is necessary for a complete and thorough confession.[16] The most important act in penance is contrition, which must be joined to a firm purpose of amendment. Contrition must be genuine, i.e., it must be a sincere conversion of will, a moral negation of sin founded in the will, an aversion to sin. It need not, of necessity, be experienced by feeling; incidental emotion is good but not essential nor necessary for we do not always have control over our emotions. Contrition is fundamentally a matter of the will. It is a resolute turning away from sin, with the wish not to have sinned at all and the determined will not to sin again. Contrition has to be supernatural, i.e., it must proceed from the motives taught us by faith. We distinguish between perfect contrition which springs from a soul that loves God with a childlike love, and imperfect contrition which sees in God only a severe judge and vindicator of justice. Perfect contrition eradicates sin directly because love for God and mortal sin are as mutually repugnant as light and darkness. However, the obligation to confess the mortal sin remains; as a matter of fact, perfect contrition includes the resolve to confess the sin. Imperfect contrition is sufficient for a worthy reception of the sacrament of Penance. In such reception the sacrament, by bringing the penitent in touch with Christ and His redemptive

[16] In examining our conscience we should be vigilant, but not to such an extent that we become distraught. Should we have forgotten a grievous sin, it is forgiven us, although the obligation still remains to confess it when it is again remembered.

work, infuses into his heart sanctifying grace and the state of love for God. Now, since love has thus entered the heart of the penitent, the remembrance of his sin, vivified by the infused love of God, will have the quality of perfect contrition. Previous to his reception of the sacrament, the penitent, in the hypothesis of imperfect contrition, could not lift his heart to God with a sincere and child-like love; after absolution this will be easy, since, with sanctifying grace, love dwells in his heart.

The actual confession of sins must be entire, sincere, and clear. It is entire when, so far as is possible, one confesses at least all his mortal sins together with their number and the circumstances affecting the nature of the sin (e.g., theft from a church). Conscious omission of a mortal sin renders the confession unworthy. An unworthy confession, and consequently all intervening confessions, must be repeated worthily. In this connection it is well to remember that we are not obliged to confess venial sins.

Satisfaction is atonement for the order disturbed by sin and for the consequent insult to God. It is imposed by the priest. According to present custom, ordinarily it consists of special prayers; in ancient times, however, penances were very severe and were, as a rule, performed publicly. If a sin is in any way injurious to other human beings, the perpetrator is obliged to repair the injury done so far as he is able. The validity of confession requires at least the will to make satisfaction. If its performance were afterward omitted, the confession remains valid notwithstanding, but if the omission were deliberate, then a new sin would be committed. Satisfaction, like confession, is a service to the community. The objective order disturbed by sin has to be restored in accordance with the judgment of the priest who is the representative of the community (the Church).

Penance, we have said, was instituted after the fashion of a judicial trial. At a trial, the judge must be competent, and the accused must be subject to him. How does this apply to penance? An individual penitent is not the subject of every priest, nor is every priest the competent judge for every individual. For example, I owe reverence to every bishop as a successor of the Apostles; yet I am bound in actual obedience to my own bishop only. This specification of authority or competency is determined by "approbation"; the priest has "jurisdiction" (power to administer justice) in the territory for which he has been approved (generally his own diocese).

From our foregoing discussion we can conclude that the effects of the sacrament of penance are the following: it confers or increases sanctifying grace; it remits sin and eternal punishment and at least a part of the temporal punishments due to sin; and it conveys special actual grace. By penance all the merits and virtues previously acquired, but which were destroyed by mortal sin, are now restored to the penitent.

We append here a brief discussion of the doctrine of indulgences. An *indulgence* is a remission of the temporal punishment due to sins (which have already been forgiven), but it is never a remission of sin itself. The Church, by reason of her power to remit or retain, has in our times substituted lighter penances for the more severe ones of primitive discipline. To those performing these penances she grants a share in the merits of Christ and the saints, over which she has the right of disposal. To gain any indulgence, the state of sanctifying grace is required. There are two kinds of indulgences, partial and plenary. A plenary indulgence is the remission of all the punishment due to sin, while a partial indulgence is the remission of only a part of the punishment. To illustrate: an indulgence of seven years is the equivalent in merit to seven years of the former practice of public penance. To gain a plenary indulgence, there is generally prescribed, over and above the respective good work, reception of the sacraments of penance and the Eucharist,[17] a visit to the Church, and prayer according to the intention of the Holy Father. Most indulgences can be applied to departed souls (to a definite person only after the manner of suffrage).[18]

5. HOLY ORDERS

Holy Orders confers on the recipient the powers of the priesthood and the grace to lead a priestly life. The full priestly power resides in the bishop; he is *the* priest in the full sense of the word. The fullness of his power is divided, as it were, among subordinate priests and inferior ministers so that they may assist him. Thus Holy Orders is a sacrament which embraces various grades. Whether all the various grades found in the Western Church today belong to the sacrament of orders has not yet been determined. At present, it is customary to consider the four minor orders (those of Ostiary, Lector, Exorcist, Acolyte) and the subdiaconate as sacramentals instituted by the Church. Most of the Eastern Churches enumerate fewer, and some of them different orders. But the Diaconate, Priesthood, and Episcopacy definitely belong to the sacrament of holy orders.

[17] As a rule, confession is required only if a grievous sin has been committed. If confession is prescribed for some special occasion (jubilee indulgence), it is of obligation even though there are only venial sins to confess. In other cases, indulgences can be gained regularly by those who confess twice a month, or communicate daily.

[18] All extremes in the matter of indulgences should be avoided. On the one hand we should not despise them; on the other hand, we should not overestimate them.

The power of the priesthood properly consists in the power to consecrate, i.e., to change bread and wine into the Body and Blood of Christ and thereby to re-enact on the altar the sacrifice of Christ. Furthermore, to the priesthood belongs the power to administer the sacraments, in particular to forgive sins, to consecrate and bless. The bishop can and does communicate this power of the priesthood to others. The deacon (minister) assists the priest at the Holy Sacrifice of the Mass, reads the Gospel, and can, with special permission, distribute Holy Communion and administer solemn baptism. The subdeacon reads the Epistle and assists at Holy Mass in a subordinate position. The office of Acolyte (escort, attendant) consists in those functions which today a Mass server performs; the exorcist undertakes the expulsion of devils (exorcism).[19] The lector (reader) reads the writings of the Church Fathers, etc., at divine services (outside of Holy Mass);[20] the ostiary (porter) is the "custodian of the door." At one time the ostiary had the charge of guarding the church entrance so that no unqualified person should intrude at the divine service. These orders are at present merely preliminary steps to the priesthood. Preceding all orders we have the sacramental of "tonsure," which signifies admission into the rank of ecclesiastics (clerics).

The minister of holy orders is the bishop.[21] Those orders which are known to constitute the sacrament, Diaconate, Priesthood, Episcopacy, are conferred by the imposition of hands. This is the ancient manner of conferring orders, as

[19] The rite of exorcism is seldom performed today, and then only with the express permission of the bishop.

[20] During Mass also, if, as on Ember days, there are other Scripture readings besides the Epistle.

[21] Minor orders can also be conferred by other dignitaries, although they bear only the sacerdotal character (cardinals, abbots, etc.)

Holy Scripture testifies in the case of the Apostles. It is a most apt way of indicating that the office conferred comes from above and not from the people or any earthly power. The order is derived from Christ, through the mediation of the Apostles and their successors. This bond proceeds in an unbroken succession from Christ to the Apostles to the bishops and down to each and every priest and cleric of today. Moreover, in the conferring of these orders, the hands of the priest are anointed with oil, the head and hands of the bishop with chrism. The priesthood was instituted by Christ at the Last Supper when He gave His Apostles the power and the commission to consecrate bread and wine in remembrance of Him.

Holy orders imprints an indelible character on the soul.[22] This means, as was stated above, a participation in the priesthood of Christ. The officiating priest receives thereby the power to administer, as an instrument of Christ and in His name, the sacraments instituted by Him for the sanctification of mankind and especially to consecrate bread and wine and thus to offer the Sacrifice of the Mass. Since consecration is achieved by an act of the will, which is outwardly manifested in words,[23] the indelible character confers on the will of the priest the power to be an instrument of the will of Christ.

According to the will of Christ, the development and the perfection of our supernatural life is closely related to the officiating priesthood. The priest is the father of the faithful, a fact which makes him, independent of his person, vener-

[22] This is true at least of those orders that comprise the sacrament.

[23] The words of consecration are therefore not a magic formula that would produce their effect mechanically, independently of the will of the one who pronounces them. The consecration is actually effected by an act of the will. Since this is elicited by a human being and has essentially a social significance, it must be given expression in words.

able, "reverend." The dignity of his office naturally imposes a serious responsibility on the priest. His office, according to what has been said before about "graces of state," is for him an occasion of humility rather than of pride. Consequently nothing is more repugnant than pride in the priest. Every priest remains in virtue of his office a representative and an instrument of Christ. This is especially true in the case of a bishop. Our attitude and disposition toward Christ can never be separated from the attitude and disposition we bear toward the individual priest or bishop.

6. MATRIMONY

Matrimony, as instituted by the Creator in Paradise, is the lawful spiritual and bodily union of man and woman for a permanent life companionship. Genesis, the first book of Holy Scriptures, relates that God gave woman to the first man as a companion and helpmate. Full of joy, Adam cried out under the inspiration of God Himself: "This is now bone of my bones, and flesh of my flesh. . . . Wherefore a man shall leave his father and mother, and shall cleave to his wife, and they shall be two in one flesh" (Gen. 2:23–24; cf. Matt. 19:4, 5). The essence of matrimony, then, consists in the union of "two in one," i.e., the complete, indissoluble spiritual-corporeal union of *one* man and *one* woman. These two fundamental characteristics of marriage, unity and indissolubility, are attached by the will of the Creator to the very nature of matrimony: "They shall be *two* in *one* flesh." "What therefore God has joined together, let no man put asunder" (Matt. 19:6, 7). This original unity and indissolubility were not always observed in the Old Testament. Taking into consideration the weaknesses of His chosen people, who had as yet not experienced the effects of the Redemption, God permitted a relaxation of His primitive ordinance.[24]

Christ restored matrimony to its original purity. On one occasion the Pharisees approached Him with the question: "Is it lawful for a man to put away his wife for any cause?" But he answered and said to them: "Have you not read that the Creator, from the beginning, made them male and female, and said: 'For this cause a man shall leave his father and mother, and cleave to his wife, and the two shall become one flesh'? Therefore, now they are no longer two, but one flesh. What therefore God has joined together, let no man put asunder." They said to Him: "Why then did Moses command to give a written notice of dismissal, and to put her away?" He said to them: "Because Moses by reason of the hardness of your heart, permitted you to put away your wives; but it was not so from the beginning. And I say to you, that whoever puts away his wife, except for immorality, and marries another, commits adultery; and he who marries a woman who has been put away commits adultery" (Matt. 19:3–9). Moses had therefore permitted the lesser evil in order to check indiscriminate divorce. Christ, however, again demands the original purity of marriage from *all* men, and forbids all divorce. Separation is permitted in case of adultery, but even then a remarriage is not allowed. "Everyone who puts away his wife and marries another commits adultery; and he who marries a woman who has been put away from her husband commits adultery" (Luke 16:18).[25]

[24] Relative to the unity of marriage, some of the Church Fathers think that God, so to say, "dispensed" the Patriarchs after the deluge and permitted them to have a number of wives so that the human race might propagate more rapidly.

[25] It is not absolutely certain that the unity and indissolubility of marriage can be known without the aid of supernatural revelation. We can say that natural reason at least recommends it very highly.

From its very beginning, marriage had a sacred character, attested to by the practices of all peoples. The encyclical *Arcanum* of Leo XIII (Feb. 10, 1880) and the *Casti Conubii* of Pius XI (Dec. 31, 1930) teach us that the Incarnation of the Son of God is implied in a mysterious manner in the marriage of Adam and Eve. The symbolical sanctity of marriage was raised to a new plane when Christ raised marriage to the dignity of a *sacrament*. This doctrine, which the Council of Trent taught explicitly, has always been the doctrine of the teaching Church. One passage of Scripture especially was always interpreted in this sense. It is an excerpt from the letter of St. Paul to the Ephesians: "Husbands, love your wives, just as Christ also loved the Church, and delivered himself up for her, that he might sanctify her. . . . Even thus ought husbands also to love their wives as their own bodies. He who loves his own wife, loves himself. . . . 'For this reason a man shall leave his father and mother, and shall cleave to his wife; and the two shall become one flesh.' This is a great mystery — *I mean in reference to Christ and to the Church*" (Eph. 5:25–32). St. Paul says, therefore, that matrimony is a holy sign, a symbol of the union between Christ and the Church. Furthermore, since Christ insisted on the pristine purity of marriage, we can presume that He confers special powers and graces so that this command might be met. Consequently, we have in marriage a holy sign conferring grace, i.e., a sacrament, as tradition has consistently affirmed. "Because God has joined them, grace dwells in those who have been joined by God" (Origen, d. 254). We can sum up the profound meaning of marriage by saying that it is a symbol of the grace-laden surrender of Christ to His Church, and since it is a sacramental sign, it confers the graces it symbolizes.

Matrimony is a sacrament not only when it is being conferred, but, according to St. Robert Bellarmine whose words Pius XI has made his own, "also while it remains; for as long as the married parties are alive so long is their union a sacrament of Christ and the Church." Matrimony does not impress an indelible character on the soul, and hence, with the death of one of the parties, the sacrament has an end. Nevertheless, it can be compared to those sacraments which impress an indelible mark, in so far as it exists beyond the moment of its performance. The inner and spiritual meaning of matrimony is realized in the divinely willed activities of the marital union, the "two in one" union which symbolizes the union between Christ and the Church. In the manifestation and rendering of marital love husband and wife obtain grace for one another. Through communal life marriage becomes a means of mutual perfection and sanctification; it is this manifestation of marital love that draws God's special graces upon this union. According to its very nature, matrimony has still another purpose, and that is the procreation of children, which Pius XI, together with St. Augustine, calls the "first blessing of marriage." For "indeed the Creator of the human race Himself, who in His goodness wished to use men as His helpers in the propagation of life, taught this when, instituting marriage in Paradise, He said to our first parents, and through them to all future spouses: 'Increase and multiply, and fill the earth' " (*Casti Conubii*). Just as the union between Christ and His Church is essentially fruitful, so must Christian marriage, the symbol of His union, have an essential relation to offspring. The child thus becomes a new bond of union between man and wife. The primary purpose of the spiritual-corporeal union of the sexes is therefore the child. A secondary purpose of marriage is the regulation of the sexual impulses.

The contracting parties themselves confer the sacrament of matrimony on one another. The external sign of the sacrament is the outwardly expressed contract, signifying mutual surrender and acceptance. Christian marriage is a valid marriage contract raised to the dignity of a sacrament. Among Christians the marriage contract and the sacrament of matrimony are inseparable and are, in fact, identical. So soon as a Christian man and a Christian woman give their consent, a consent which is recognized as valid by the Church, at that very moment the contracting parties confer the sacrament upon each other.

The Church does not recognize a divorce in the commonly accepted sense of the term. Separation of man and wife is permissible, but so long as both parties are still living, remarriage is prohibited. Only a marriage which has been contracted but not consummated can be dissolved and then only in certain definite circumstances. The same holds good for the marriage of two nonbaptized persons in case one party is later baptized and the other party as a consequence thereupon creates difficulties that militate against a continued harmonious marital life.[26]

Because of the holy and sacramental nature of marriage, only the Church is competent to establish marriage laws. "Since marriage is by its nature something holy, it is appropriate that marriage be ruled and ordered not by the authority of princes (secular powers) but by the divine authority of the Church, who alone is the divinely appointed teacher in holy things" (*Arcanum*). For this reason the new

---

[26] This is called the Pauline privilege, because it rests on the authority of St. Paul (cf. I Cor. 7:12–15).

Code of Canon Law (1918) has determined that the "marriage of the baptized is regulated not only by divine but also by ecclesiastical law; civil power is competent for the purely civil effects of marriage" (Can. 1016). These civil effects refer to dowry, community of goods, income of widows, status in society, rights of heritage, etc. Civil power is competent, at the most, for the marriage of nonbaptized. At the same time, however, it may not make regulations that are not sanctioned by the laws of nature.

Concerning the validity of marriage, the Church has decreed at the Council of Trent that only those marriages are valid which have been contracted in the presence of the pastor and two witnesses.[27] Furthermore, from time immemorial the Church has recognized a number of so-called impediments, some of which render a marriage impossible (*diriment impediments*) and others make it illicit (*hindering impediments*). Civil legislation has also as a rule recognized these impediments. The most important diriment impediments are certain degrees of blood relationship and affinity, as well as disparity of cult, i.e., marriage between a baptized and a nonbaptized person. The most important hindering impediment is difference in religious beliefs, i.e., "a mixed marriage," marriage between a Catholic and a baptized non-Catholic.[28] For weighty reasons, the Church dispenses from some diriment and hindering impediments.

[27] The Church did not thereby alter the essence of the sacrament. She merely placed a *sine qua non* condition for the validity of the contract. Pastor here also includes priests properly delegated by him.

[28] The chief reasons against mixed marriages are: (1) the danger of indifference (i.e., the opinion that all religions are equally good) for the Catholic spouse and for the children, (2) danger of disrupting marital harmony, (3) possible tragedy resulting from the non-Catholic's nonbelief in the indissolubility of marriage.

7. EXTREME UNCTION

Extreme unction is that sacrament in which a sick person receives the grace of God for the salvation of his soul and oftentimes also for the welfare of his body as well. It is administered by anointing with oil the eyes, the ears, the nose, the mouth, the hands, and the feet. During the action of anointing, the following words are spoken: "Through this holy unction and His own most tender mercy, may the Lord pardon thee whatever faults thou hast committed by sight, hearing, etc." In Holy Scripture, unction is mentioned in the letter of St. James. "Is any one among you sick? Let him bring in the presbyters of the Church, and let them pray over him, anointing him with oil in the name of the Lord. And the prayer of faith will save the sick man, and the Lord will raise him up, and if he be in sins, they shall be forgiven him" (James 5:14, 15). Hence the sacrament of extreme unction is of divine institution.

In this passage the effects of holy unction are clearly expressed. The word "save" refers primarily to the salvation of the soul, a happy death. This sacred anointing relieves the soul of the final dross of its earthly existence. Extreme unction increases, moreover, sanctifying grace, and may also confer it in case the sick man can no longer go to confession; it destroys sin and removes either fully, or in part, the punishment due to sins. Finally it takes away the remains of sins already forgiven (attachment to earthly things, bad habits). By "salvation" we can also understand the health of the body, which extreme unction imparts if it should be to the spiritual good of the sick person. It is noteworthy how much this effect is emphasized in the prayers that accompany the administration of this sacrament.[29] "The Lord will raise him up." Unction imparts strength in sufferings and temptations, and gives patience and confidence. In the struggle of death, extreme unction gives strength to the soul especially. Extreme unction can be received only by one in danger of death from illness and can be administered only once during the same period of illness. If the danger from the same or another illness recurs, the sacrament should and can be received again.

*   *   *

To recapitulate, we see how the sacramental life of the Church accompanies man from the cradle to the grave. All states and important stages of life are sanctified and filled with the life of the Incarnate Son of God unto the one end: "The mature measure of the fullness of Christ" (Eph. 4:13), the consummation of all things in Him.

---

[29] It is wise not to delay the administration of extreme unction until such time when there is no longer any hope for recovery. We have no right to expect miraculous cures, but rather we expect that God will utilize the sacrament to strengthen the natural faculties of man. The sick person should be able to follow the administration of the sacrament intelligently; in this way we can expect the graces of the sacrament to become more fruitfully operative.

CHAPTER IX

THE CONSUMMATION

1. DEATH AND PARTICULAR JUDGMENT

"IT IS appointed unto men to die once but after this comes the judgment" (Heb. 9:27). Death is the common lot of all the children of Adam.[1] "For as in Adam all die, so in Christ all will be made to live" (I Cor. 15:22). Death is the most terrifying and most evident effect of sin. "Through one man sin entered into the world and through sin death, and thus death has passed into all men because all have sinned" (Rom. 5:12).

Death brings our temporal, earthly life to an end. But, as our faith teaches, death is not the end of all things, but merely a transition into another, an immortal life. Death is immediately followed by the particular judgment, which decides the eternal lot of man.[2] This, in turn, will depend on just what was the state of affairs of our earthly life. Time

[1] It is a moot question in theology whether those persons living at the second coming of Christ will have to die. St. Paul seems to hold the contrary point of view: "We who live, who survive, shall be caught up together with them in clouds to meet the Lord in the air, and so we shall ever be with the Lord" (I Thess. 4:17).

[2] The fact that there can be no conversion after death lies in the very nature of the separation of soul and body, and is fully in accord with the teachings of philosophy. Conversion of will must somehow be associated with a corresponding bodily activity and is conditioned by it.

and eternity are therefore not two wholly separated spheres; they stand in a similar relation to each other as the sowing to the reaping, the seed to the·plant. Time should be a preparation for eternity. Nothing is known of the manner in which the particular judgment will be held. The liturgy (in the sequence *Dies irae* from the Mass for the dead) poetically employs the figure of a book in which is recorded all that man did on earth. St. Augustine explains this book as a divine light, "by which each one recalls his good and evil deeds" (*De civitate Dei,* Lib. 20, cap. 14).

It is most important to understand eternal life as a definite state of being. But since our bodies are to share finally in life eternal, it is certain also that they will inhabit a definite place.

2. ETERNAL DEATH

One who does not die in the state of sanctifying grace, in whose soul there is not the radiance and the light of which we have spoken, is spiritually dead and has no life in him. Because he has consciously rejected the Saviour from whom alone salvation could come, he is dead for all eternity.

The eternal duration of the punishments of hell is a doctrine established beyond all doubt. Christ says: "Depart from me, accursed ones, into the everlasting fire" (Matt. 25:41). He speaks of the "unquenchable fire, where the worm dies not, and the fire is not quenched" (Mark 9:45). The few Church writers (Origen, d. 254, Gregory of Nyssa, d. after 394), who held that all the damned would at some time return to salvation, were vehemently opposed even by their contemporaries. Human beings so easily find sentimental difficulties with this dogma. It must always be remembered that the one delivered over to eternal damnation has consciously and stubbornly rejected the grace of God, and has hardened his heart to a hatred of God. In this hatred of God he will persist for all eternity.

In short, an inner disruption and the exclusion of divine life is the essential punishment of hell. Theoretically, of course, the damned recognize that God is the Supreme Good. However, because of their spiritual death, He stands opposed to them, and hence they are driven to hate Him. They are thus the victims of an everlasting internal dissension. They are also aware of the happiness of the blessed, and realize that they themselves are excluded from this happiness for all eternity. To these essential torments are added positive pains, which have been designated by the name of "hell-fire." In what this "hell-fire" consists is unknown, but it is doubtlessly different from earthly fire. One thing is certain: the bodies of the damned after resurrection will have to endure pains. The pains of hell differ in degree. Accordingly, he who committed more grievous sins will be punished more severely.

Those who die in the state of grievous sin are condemned to the punishments of hell; or rather, the punishments of hell are the natural and necessary consequences of the absence of sanctifying grace and love of God in the soul of the sinner. For that reason, the same lot befalls those who die in original sin. If, however, in the latter case, there is not the further guilt of actual sin, then the individual will only be punished by the loss of the vision of God and not by positive punishment. Nothing has been expressly revealed in regard to the destiny of children who die without baptism. This much only is certain — that they will not be admitted to the vision of God. The Council of Florence (1438–45) has defined that even those who die in the state of original sin only cannot enter the kingdom of heaven. The same truth can be deduced from the necessity of infant baptism. We have no reason at all to deny that a natural state of happiness is in store for children who die without baptism. This is the view favored by St. Thomas Aquinas.[3]

The existence of hell brings home to us with terrifying clarity the fact that God is *just,* and that His justice is not to be separated from His mercy. We must stress with special emphasis, however, that hell is not a blind destiny into which the sinner plunges unawares, but is his self-chosen and fully deserved portion.

3. ETERNAL LIFE

One departing this life as a living member of the Body of Christ, as a living branch of the vine, which is Christ, cannot be lost eternally, but will possess eternal life. True it is that most men at the moment of death are not sufficiently purified to enjoy immediately the pure and holy vision of God. There exists a state of purification to which these souls must go. They will undergo purification, we may say, willingly and readily, because they realize the vast distance between themselves and the all-holy God. This state and place is called purgatory. The Church has made no official decision whatever concerning the nature of purgatory; the Eastern Churches, even those in communion with Rome, avoid the term "fire" in connection with purgatory. But the existence of a place of purification is not only in accord with reason but is expressly revealed as well. In the Old Testament we read: "It is therefore a holy and wholesome thought to pray for the dead, that they may be loosed from sins" (II Macc

[3] The place where the infants, dying without baptism, go, is called "Limbo," i.e., threshold of the nether world.

12:46).[4] For that reason Judas Macchabeus ordered sacrifice to be offered in Jerusalem for those who had been slain and on whom pagan and idolatrous votive gifts had been found. It is certain that the suffering of the "poor souls" is very great and that they suffer without being able to gain further merits, i.e., to grow in charity. Most severe of all is the fact that they are excluded from the vision of God. It is a further certainty that we can come to their aid by prayer and especially by sacrifice (Holy Mass). But it is equally certain that they know of their eternal salvation and that they derive great comfort therefrom. Consequently, purgatory is decidedly a place of love and surrender to the will of God. After the soul has completed its period of purgation, or if it departed this life free from the last stain of sin or obligation to temporal punishment, it enters into the eternal bliss of heaven.

After a thorough investigation into the exemplary life and death of an individual, the Church occasionally proclaims through her infallible teaching authority, that such a person has attained the happiness of heaven and is worthy of being venerated as a saint. It is spiritually advantageous to honor and imitate the virtues of the saints and to pray to them for their intercession (veneration of saints). As a matter of historical fact, the primitive Church thus honored her martyrs and also, since the fourth century, other pious and saintly persons. The practice of honoring the relics and images of these saints is equally as ancient and natural. The veneration thus paid is directed to the saints and not to inanimate objects.

The happiness of heaven consists essentially in the vision

---

[4] After the Vulgate. This passage sounds a little different in the original text but it has the same meaning.

of God. It is very difficult, of course, for earthly minded men
to conceive what heaven really is; it is, however, sufficient to
say that it is the essential bliss and happiness of God Himself. The beatific vision is a complete immersion of the soul
in God, while still retaining its own personality; it is a participation in the life of the Most Holy Trinity. Thus shall
we be drawn wholly into the inner life of the Father, the
Son, and the Holy Spirit. God's happiness will be ours to
share. As the beatitude of God consists essentially in the
knowledge and love of Himself, or of the three persons one
for another, so, too, we shall know God as He is (and in Him
know all creation), and love Him for all eternity. We shall
no longer labor under intellectual difficulties and bodily
afflictions. "God will wipe away every tear from their eyes.
And death shall be no more; neither shall there be mourn-
ing, nor crying, nor pain any more" (Apoc. 21:4). "We see
now through a mirror in an obscure manner, but then face
to face. Now I know in part, but then I shall know even as I
have been known" (I Cor. 13:12). "Eye has not seen nor ear
heard, nor has it entered into the heart of man, what things
God has prepared for those that love Him" (I Cor. 2:9).

Even creature benefits belong to the bliss of heaven,
such as friendship with other blessed spirits, reunion with
our loved ones, and especially the glory of the body. All
those who are united with Christ will rise blessed and glorified. "Our citizenship is in heaven from which also we
eagerly await a Saviour, our Lord Jesus Christ, who will re-
fashion the body of our lowliness, conforming it to the body
of his glory by exerting the power by which he is able also
to subject all things to himself" (Phil. 3:20, 21). As a pledge
of our resurrection the Saviour has given us the Holy
Eucharist; Christ's own resurrection was the cause: "Christ

has risen from the dead, the first fruits of those who have fallen asleep. For since by a man came death, by a man also comes resurrection of the dead. For as in Adam all die, so in Christ all will be made to live" (I Cor. 15:20–22).

The beatific vision likewise admits of degrees; he who loves God more will have a greater share in Him. Yet each one will be completely satisfied with his lot, as two persons of varied intellectual attainments derive full (although unequal) satisfaction in the contemplation of a work of art. In its eternal beatitude, human nature will also experience its full perfection. The complete and final development of the powers implanted in human nature by the Creator, whether these be depth of knowledge or any other object of legitimate striving, shall be realized in the surrender of the soul into the life of God.

The Saviour Himself was wont to picture eternal bliss as a joyous banquet, a marriage feast, a return to the father's house. In these similitudes another essential feature of eternal beatitude appears which is today too easily overlooked. This is the happiness of the holy *community* of the Church Triumphant. Just as man's personal sanctity is based upon its fructifying within the community of the Church; so too eternity equally perfects the community and *in it* the individual.

4. THE GENERAL JUDGMENT

At the end of all time, the general judgment of the world will take place. Above all, this judgment has an historical significance. By it, the real meaning of history shall be made manifest. History is "God's eternal plan for mankind as it was accomplished in the course of time, during which God prepared for Himself through Christ an adequate veneration and glorification proceeding from the free homage of man himself" (John Adam Möhler). The universal judgment will reveal Christ as the divinely appointed king and the center of the world. Truth will triumph over all falsehood, the good of right will vanquish all the cruelty of might. Just as God created all things in His Son, and as the Son of God is the epitome of all creation, so shall the Incarnate Son of God, Jesus Christ, be proclaimed the center of the whole universe. "For in Him were created all things in the heavens and on the earth, things visible and things invisible . . . all things have been created through and unto him [i.e., for him] and he is before all creatures, and in him all things hold together" (Col. 1:16–18). Men shall, at the end of time, acknowledge Christ as their rightful King; the folly of those who abandoned Him and denied Him shall be revealed. It shall then be demonstrated to the entire world that the real meaning and purpose of creation is summed up in Christ: the Son of God, who united creation to Himself in the microcosm, man, and who by leading man back to God rendered Him the homage and honor which is His due as the Creator. Not only shall the insufficiency of mere nature be fully known, but its elevation and perfection in the supernatural shall be made manifest.

Prior to the general judgment, fearful things will come to pass. It would seem that the history of Christ living on in the Church is to follow the same course taken by His life on earth. Christ (in the Church) will again be crucified and killed; yet precisely in these seeming defeats will lie the victory of His glorious Resurrection. Indeed, Christ triumphs through His death; His apparent overthrow is but the beginning of His glorious triumph.

Holy Scripture speaks in figures of the signs to foreshadow

the judgment. These signs are so clear, however, that they give us a good general idea of those times. The following facts are sketched in graphic, plain terms.

First, fearful catastrophes will come upon the world. "For you shall hear of wars and rumors of wars. Take care that you do not be alarmed, for these things must come to pass, but the end is not yet. For nation will rise against nation, and kingdom against kingdom; and there will be pestilences and famines and earthquakes in various places. But all these things are the beginnings of sorrows" (Matt. 24:6–8).

Second, there will be a great defection from Christ, with evil on the increase. Toward the end of time, the powers opposing Christ will appear, united, as it were, in one man (the "Anti-Christ"). "We beseech you, brethren, by the coming of our Lord Jesus Christ and our being gathered together unto Him, not to be hastily shaken from your right mind . . . as though the day of the Lord were near at hand . . . for the day of the Lord will not come unless the apostasy comes first, and the man of sin is revealed, the son of perdition, who opposes and is exalted above all that is called God, or that is worshipped, so that he sits in the temple of God and gives himself out as if he were God . . . for the mystery of iniquity is already at work" (II Thess. 2:1–7). Anti-Christ will make his appearance in the garb of a just man; in his claims he will even appeal to Christ. In this manner will the opponents of Christ exercise a seductive power. "False Christs and false prophets will arise, and will show great signs and wonders, so as to lead astray, if possible, even the elect" (Matt. 24:24). "His (the Anti-Christ's) coming is according to the working of Satan with all power and signs and lying wonders, and with all wicked deception to those who are perishing. For they have not received the love of truth that they might be saved. Therefore God sends them a misleading influence that they may believe falsehood" (II Thess. 2:9–11).

Third, strange phenomena in the heavens shall frighten mankind. "Immediately after the tribulation of those days, the sun will be darkened, and the moon will not give her light, and the stars will fall from heaven, and the powers of heaven will be shaken. And then will appear the sign of the Son of Man in heaven" (Matt. 24:29, 30).

Finally, Christ will appear in the heavens wondrous and glorious, knowable to all and the cynosure of all the world. The dead will rise again, and the judgment of Christ will separate the wicked from the good, the former to be delivered over to eternal pain, the latter to share everlasting bliss. "Then will appear the sign of the Son of Man in heaven; and then will all tribes of the earth mourn, and they will see the Son of Man coming upon the clouds of heaven with great power and majesty. For as the lightning comes forth from the east and shines even to the west, so also will the coming of the Son of Man be. And He will send forth his angels with a trumpet and a great sound, and they will gather his elect from the four winds, from end to end of the heavens" (Matt. 24:27, 30, 31). "The hour is coming in which all who are in the tombs shall hear the voice of the Son of God. And they who have done good shall come forth unto resurrection of life; but they who have done evil unto resurrection of judgment" (John 5:28, 29). "The Son of Man is to come with his angels in the Glory of his Father, and then he will render to everyone according to his conduct" (Matt. 16:27). "When the Son of Man shall come in his majesty, and all the angels with him, then he will sit on the throne of his glory; and before him will be gathered, all the nations and he will separate them one from another, as the shepherd separates the sheep from the goats" (Matt. 25:31, 33). Then will come the victory of good, the triumph of all those who cling to Christ. "When these things begin to come to pass, look up, and lift up your heads, because your redemption is at hand" (Luke 21:28). "The Lord Jesus will slay (that wicked one) with the breath of his mouth and will destroy him with the brightness of his coming" (II Thess. 2:8).

Christ will transform and renew heaven and earth. "The heavens that now are, and the earth . . . have been stored up, being reserved for fire against the day of judgment and destruction of ungodly men. . . . The heavens, being on fire, will be dissolved and the elements will melt away by reason of the heat of the fire! But we look for new heavens and a new earth, according to his promises, wherein dwells justice" (II Pet. 3:7, 12, 13). Then surely shall have been heard the petition: "Thy kingdom come!"

Actually the judgment of the world is already taking place. It began with the appearance of Christ, who is the Great Winnower of all souls, good and bad. And the judgment precisely consists in no more than this winnowing. John the Baptist has already described Him with a fan in his hand, separating the chaff from the wheat (Matt. 3:12; Luke 3:17). The history of the world has no meaning other than to complete this separation, and to declare victorious the cause of the kingdom of Christ over the kingdom of evil. Any wavering between the two is impossible: "He who is not with me is against me, and he who does not gather with me scatters" (Matt. 12:30). Victory shall certainly come to the kingdom of Christ. When the time is full, then does Christ come as the judge of the world: "Neither does the Father judge any man, but all judgment he has given to the Son, that all men may honor the Son even as they honor the Father" (John 5:22, 23). And so the "last day" becomes the "day of Christ" of which St. Paul so often speaks. God the Father has, indeed, given the world to Him, hence from it the glory of Christ should come forth. With the Last Judgment by Christ the history of the world will be concluded; on that day He will manifest Himself as the real end, the true meaning of all creation. If, as was said above, all things find their true meaning only in man, the microcosm, then this is chiefly and completely true of the God-Man only. Christ it is who gives meaning to history, gives meaning to art, to invention and science, to the state and to every human society, to the natural and to the supernatural. Christ will at length return His kingdom to the Father, so that in the end all things may redound to the glory of God, the Father.

"Then comes the end, when he [Christ] delivers the kingdom to God the Father, when he does away with all sovereignty, authority, and power. For he must reign, until 'he has put all his enemies under his feet' (Ps. 109:1). And the last enemy to be destroyed will be death, for 'he has put all things under his feet' (Ps. 8:8) . . . And when all things are made subject to him, then the Son himself will also be made subject to him who subjected all things to him, that

"GOD MAY BE ALL IN ALL"

(I Cor. 15:24-28.)

APPENDIX I

The various degrees of theological certitude are: (*a*)
Dogma (*D*), an article of faith; (*b*) Certain (*Cert.*), i.e., the
unanimous teaching of theologians; (*c*) Commonly accepted
(*Com. Acc.*), i.e., taught by the majority of theologians; (*d*)
Probable (*Prob.*), i.e., held by distinguished theologians.

INTRODUCTION

The extraordinary teaching authority resides in the pope and in the General Council (*D*).

The sources of faith are Sacred Scripture and Tradition (*D*). Holy Scripture is inspired, i.e., it has God for its author. (*D*). Holy Scripture is free from error (*Cert*.) (Leo XIII).

Part I

God's Eternal Plan of Creation and Redemption
Chapter II: God, One and Triune

There is one God, who is the essence of all perfection. He is infinite, eternal and immutable, omnipresent and immense, omniscient and all wise, holy, good, just, merciful,

long-suffering, faithful, and true (*D*).

There is one God in three Persons. These three Persons are the Father, the Son, and the Holy Spirit. They are distinguished one from another by their various "processions": the Father proceeds from no one, the Son proceeds from the Father, and the Holy Spirit proceeds from the Father and from the Son (*D*). The procession of the Son from the Father is termed "generation" (*D*). The Son proceeds by way of mental generation from the intellect of the Father (*Cert*.). He is therefore known as the "Word" (*D*). The Holy Spirit proceeds from the mutual love existing between the Father

and Son (*Cert*.).

Chapter III: Economy of Creation and Redemption

God created the material and spiritual world out of nothing (*D*). All creatures were created good. Evil came

through the sin of the creature (*D*).

God created the angels, i.e., spirits superior to man (*D*).

The angels were created in the state of sanctifying grace, but not in the state of glory (*Cert.*). Some angels sinned (*D*). The good angels watch over mankind (*D*). Every baptized soul has his or her own guardian angel (*Cert.*). PAGE 40-41

God created man to His own image. God created man at least mediately (*D*). Every immortal soul is created by God (*Cert.*). God created the bodies of the first human beings directly (*Prob.*). All mankind descends from the first man and woman (*Cert.*). 41-42

PART II

EXECUTION OF THE PLAN OF REDEMPTION

CHAPTER IV: NECESSITY OF REDEMPTION — ORIGINAL SIN

The first persons of the human race were created in a state of justice and holiness (*D*). This state was a supernatural gift of grace (*Cert.*). The first human beings were immortal (*D*). They were not subject to inordinate desires (*Cert.*). They were not subject to suffering or ignorance (*Com. Acc.*). These endowments were "preternatural" gifts of God (*Cert.*). 49-50

The first human beings sinned grievously, in so far as they transgressed a command of God (*D*). All those who are the natural descendants of Adam (the Blessed Virgin excepted) are born with the guilt of his sin, original sin (*D*). Loss of sanctifying grace is a result of original sin (*D*). The essence of original sin consists in the loss (culpable) of sanctifying grace (*Com. Acc.*). He who dies with original sin on his soul cannot enjoy the beatific vision (*D*). 50-52

52-55

CHAPTER V: REDEMPTION

Christ is our Redeemer (*D*). Christ is true God and true Man. The divine and the human nature are united in the

PAGE
56-64 one person of Christ (*D*). Christ was born of the Virgin Mary (*D*).

Mary is the Mother of God (*D*). Mary always remained a virgin (*D*). Mary was immaculately conceived (*D*). The body of Mary was assumed into heaven (*Cert.*). Mary is the mediatrix of graces. She is mediatrix because she bore Christ (*D*), because through her intercession she can obtain every grace for us (*Cert.*), because every grace is obtained through her intercession (*Prob.*). To Mary is due 64-68 special veneration (*hyperdulia*) (*D*).

Christ redeemed the world through His death on the cross (*D*). Christ offered Himself as a true and perfect sacrifice on the cross. Hence He is *the* High Priest (*D*). Christ died for all men (*Cert.*). Christ did not die for the "predestined" or 69-72
72-76
92-98 for the faithful departed alone (*D*). Christ made superabundant satisfaction for sin (*Cert.*). Christ arose from the dead (*D*). Christ is the head of all mankind (*Cert.*).

Part III

Application of the Redemption — Our Sanctification
CHAPTER VI: GOD, THE SANCTIFIER

Sanctification is pre-eminently ascribed to the Holy Spirit. He is the Spirit of the Son of God made Man. Hence, He is also the Spirit of all those who partake of the Sonship of God through incorporation into Christ. The Holy Spirit dwells in the Christian who is a living member of the Body of 79-85 Christ (*Com. Acc.*).

The sanctification of man consists in the infusion of sanctifying grace, which is a permanent state of the soul, destroys 85 sin (*D*), and makes us partakers "of the divine nature" (*Cert.*).

Man is also in need of "actual grace," i.e., a temporary help from God (*D*). Grace is absolutely necessary to salvation (*D*). The beginning of justification is also from God (*D*). Every just person receives sufficient grace for the observance of the commandments, provided he does not make himself unworthy of these graces (*D*). God gives sinners sufficient grace for conversion (*Com. Acc.*). Every nonbeliever receives sufficient grace to attain faith (*Cert.*).

85-88

Good works merit an increase in sanctifying grace and eternal life (*D*). With sanctifying grace, the theological virtues, faith, hope, charity, are infused into the soul (*D*); likewise, the moral (cardinal) virtues (*Cert.*), and the "Gifts of the Holy Spirit" (*Com. Acc.*).

86-89

The life of grace is either hampered or destroyed by sin (*D*). Sin is the transgression of a divine command which, in the last analysis, is founded in the nature of God (*Cert.*). Mortal sin destroys the life of grace and merits eternal damnation (*D*). He commits a mortal sin who knowingly and willingly transgresses God's command in a serious matter (*Cert.*). Venial sins do not destroy the life of grace (*D*).

89-91

CHAPTER VII: THE HOLY AND SANCTIFYING COMMUNITY — THE CHURCH

Christ founded the Church for the sanctification of mankind of all times (*D*). The Church is the ever living Christ, the mystical Body of Christ (*Cert.*). The Church is one, catholic, holy, and apostolic (*D*).

92-100

CHAPTER VIII: MEANS OF GRACE — THE SACRAMENTS

A sacrament is a holy, outward sign, instituted by Christ, to give grace (*Cert.*). A sacrament is an "efficacious" sign; it effects what it symbolizes (*Com. Acc.*). There are seven sacraments, instituted by Christ: Baptism, Confirmation, Holy Eucharist, Penance, Extreme Unction, Holy Orders, and Matrimony (*D*). The external sign of the sacrament consists in the "matter" and the "form" (*Com. Acc.*). The sacraments bring us into contact with the God-Man and His work (*Com. Acc.*).

101-105

The sacraments are effective *ex opere operato;* they contain the grace they symbolize and impart it when the recipient wills to receive the sacrament, and the minister has the intention of administering it according to the mind of the Church (*D*). The validity of the sacraments does not depend on the faith or on the sanctity of the minister (*D*).

104-105

Baptism, confirmation, and holy orders imprint an "indelible character" on the soul of the recipient (*D*). This "indelible character" is a participation in the priesthood of Christ (*Com. Acc.*). The sacraments are an "externalizing" of faith (*Com. Acc.*).

106-107

There are also sacramentals which have been instituted by the Church (*Cert.*). These rites and prayers of the Church may not be held in contempt (*D*).

107-108

Baptism is a true sacrament, instituted by Christ (*D*). Baptism is the first of the sacraments (*Cert.*). Natural water is required for the administration of baptism (*D*). Baptism is administered by pouring water on the head of the one to be baptized, while saying at the same time: "I baptize thee in the name of the Father and of the Son and of the Holy Ghost." Every person can baptize validly and in case of necessity may and should do so. In ordinary circumstances, the pastor is the minister of baptism (*Cert.*). Baptism destroys the guilt of all sin: original sin and all actual sins committed before baptism, and also all punishment due for sin (*D*). Baptism imprints an indelible character (*D*). The baptismal character denotes membership in Christ and participation in His priesthood (*Cert.*). Baptism is absolutely necessary to salvation (*D*). The baptism of blood and the baptism of desire can, under certain circumstances, be substituted for the baptism of water (*Cert.*). Baptism may and should be administered to infants (*D*).

Confirmation is a true sacrament, instituted by Christ (*D*). The external sign of confirmation consists in the anointing with chrism, the accompanying imposition of hands, and the saying at the same time of the words: "I sign thee with the sign of the cross and confirm thee with the chrism of salvation in the name of the Father and of the Son and of the Holy Ghost. Amen" (*Cert.*). Confirmation also imprints an indelible character upon the soul (*D*).

The Holy Eucharist is a true sacrifice and sacrament instituted by Christ (*D*). In the Holy Eucharist, the Body and Blood of Christ are really and truly present (*D*). The manner in which Christ becomes present in the Holy Eucharist is called by the Church "transubstantiation" (*D*). Christ is present whole and entire in every part and particle of the Holy Eucharist (*D*). Christ remains present in the Holy Eucharist for as long as the appearances of bread and wine remain (*D*). Adoration is due to Christ in the Holy Eucharist (*D*).

The Mass is a true and real sacrifice (*D*). The Sacrifice of the Mass is essentially the same as that of the cross (*D*).

Holy Communion effects the remission of venial sin, and accidentally effects remission of mortal sin if the recipient be ignorant of serious guilt (*Com. Acc.*). The Holy Eucharist is a means of salvation in as much as it frees us from our daily faults (*D*). The Holy Eucharist is the pledge of our bodily resurrection (*D*).

Penance is a true sacrament, instituted by Christ for the remission of sins committed after baptism (*D*). Christ gave to His Church the power to remit all sins *without exception* committed after baptism (*D*). Only priests and bishops can administer the sacrament of penance (*D*). The external sign of penance consists in the words of the priest as "form," and the acts of the penitent as "matter" (*Com. Acc.*). (According to some the ceremonies and words of the priest alone are the matter and form.) The confession of all grievous sins according to the number and kind is required for a valid reception of penance (*D*). Auricular confession dates from the very beginning of Christianity (*D*). Contrition (with purpose of amendment) and satisfaction are required for the sacrament of penance (*Cert.*). Imperfect contrition suffices in the sacrament of penance (*Cert.*). The entire temporal punishment is not always forgiven with the guilt of sin (*D*). For the validity
125-129 of the sacrament, the minister must have "jurisdiction" (*D*).

The Church has the power to grant indulgences, and their
129-130 use is beneficial to Christians (*D*).

Holy orders is a true sacrament, instituted by Christ (*D*). Consecration of bishops and ordination of priests belong to
130 this sacrament (*D*). The diaconate also belongs (*Cert.*).

In regard to subdeacon, acolyte, exorcist, reader, and ostiary, St. Thomas is of the opinion that, in so far as they share in the order of deaconship (assistantship), they also partake of the sacrament of holy orders. However, the
130 greater number of present-day theologians hold the contrary
131 view. The ordinary minister of holy orders is the bishop (*D*). Whether the imposition of hands or the presentation of the insignia of the various orders is the exterior sign of this sacrament, has not been dogmatically defined. Most probably the essential exterior sign of the sacrament of holy orders

(bishop, priest, deacon) is the imposition of hands. Those
grades of the priesthood which belong to the sacrament of
holy orders imprint an indelible character (*D*).

Marriage, as the legitimate spiritual-corporeal union of
man and woman in a permanent life companionship, was instituted by God in paradise (*Cert.*). Christ raised marriage to
the dignity of a sacrament (*D*). Christian marriage is monog-
amous, i.e., one man and one woman bind themselves to a
life union (*D*). Christian marriage, if it has at least been
physically consummated, is indissoluble (*Cert.*). The marriage of two nonbaptized persons can be dissolved by reason
of the Pauline privilege (*Cert.*). The two contracting parties
mutually administer the sacrament to one another (*Cert.*).
The external sign of the sacrament of marriage consists in
the visibly expressed marriage contract, indicating mutual
surrender and acceptance (*Com. Acc.*). Every valid marriage
contract of two Christians is in itself a sacrament. Sacrament
and contract are inseparable (*Cert.*). Christian marriage is
subject to divine and to ecclesiastical law as well (*D*). The
Church may set up marriage impediments (*D*). The secular
power is competent in the mere civil effects of marriage (*Cert.*).

Extreme unction is a true sacrament, instituted by Christ.
The Apostle James is witness to it (*D*). The "matter" of
extreme unction consists in the anointing with holy oils
(*Cert.*). The "form" used in the Western Church is as follows: "Through this holy unction and His most tender
mercy, may the Lord pardon you whatever sins you have committed by sight, hearing, etc." The effects of extreme unction
are: strength of soul against all the trials and tribulations in
the hour of death (*Cert.*); remission of the guilt of venial sin
(*Cert.*), and mortal sin (*Com. Acc.*); the partial or entire remission of the temporal punishment due to sin, as well as

other consequences of sin (*Com. Acc.*); finally, restoration of bodily health, if this will aid the soul (*Cert.*). Extreme

unction is administered by the priest (*D*).

CHAPTER IX: THE CONSUMMATION

Every man born in the state of original sin (with the possible exception of those who are living at the second coming of Christ) must die (*D*). The soul is judged immediately

after death. Its eternal destiny remains unchanged (*Cert.*). He who dies in the state of mortal sin will be doomed to eternal punishment (*D*). The punishment of hell consists primarily in exclusion from the vision of God (*D*). To this essential punishment are added other positive punishments

(*Cert.*). The punishments of the damned vary in degree (*D*).

The souls of those who die in the state of sanctifying grace, and are still burdened with venial sin or temporal punishment due for sin, must undergo a process of purgation (*D*).

Our prayers can aid the "Poor Souls" (*D*). The saints also come to their aid (*Com. Acc.*).

Those who die without the least stain of sin or have no temporal punishment on their soul enter immediately into a state of complete supernatural beatitude (*D*). Salvation is eternal and can never be lost (*D*). Salvation consists essentially in the beatific vision (*D*). With this essential beatitude is associated the happiness attendant on the possession of

created goods, e.g., transfiguration of the body (*Com. Acc.*).

The saints in heaven are worthy of veneration. The veneration of the relics and images of saints is permissible and salutary. The saints intercede for us, and it is good and

advantageous for us to ask their intercession (*D*). At the end of time, all men will rise from the dead (*D*). Christ

will come again as judge of the world, to judge all men (*D*).

APPENDIX II

A. PROOFS FOR THE EXISTENCE OF GOD

The existence of a personal God is an absolute prerequisite for true religion. The Vatican Council (1870) has defined that the one and true creator, our Lord and "God, who is the beginning and the end of all things, can be known with certainty by the human intellect, from created things." This is likewise the express teaching of Holy Scripture. St. Paul in his letter to the Romans writes: "For since the creation of the world his invisible attributes are clearly seen — his everlasting power also and divinity — being understood through the things that are made" (Rom. 1:20). To understand the proofs for the existence of God, we must note the following:

1. Faith in God is not dependent on our ability to fathom the philosophical proofs for God's existence. Our faith consists in a supernatural certitude, engendered by the supernatural means of the grace of God that stimulates and strengthens the human will. In His revelations, especially in and through Christ, God reveals Himself much as does the sun which manifests itself by shining upon and "revealing" other things.

2. The force of conviction resulting from the proofs of God's existence is easily perceived by the sound and unspoiled human intellect. It is a more difficult matter, how-

ever, for a mind poisoned by the false philosophy that questions the ability of the mind to know anything. This tendency to skepticism was quite prevalent in the last generation
when sound principles of tradition were so easily
surrendered.

The following arguments outline in simplest detail the
more important proofs for the existence of God:

1. The cosmological (Greek, *Kosmos:* order; world) argument. Whatever has come into existence must have received
its existence from some other being; every motion requires
a mover. If this series is continued, we arrive finally at a
Being that is self-existent, a Being who received His existence from no other being but who is the cause of all other
beings, i.e., the First Unmoved Mover, God.

2. The teleological (Greek, *Telos:* "end") argument. The
universe presents the picture of a complete and well-ordered
whole. Even irrational creatures do not act without a definite
end, e.g., the bird when it builds its nest. Hence, we must
posit (place) the existence of a Being who is an intelligent
Designer and who has put order and design into all of creation. To illustrate: Obviously it would be sheer nonsense to
suppose that a masterpiece of painting, such as the *Sistine
Madonna*, has come into being by mere chance. All proofs
for the existence of God rest inevitably on the all-inclusive
and obvious principle of causation: There is no thing which
does not have an adequate cause for its existence.

The irresistible reasoning of the proofs for the existence
of God leads inexorably to a Creator who is different from
the world. Pantheism, the opinion that everything is divine
and that the world is part of the essence of God, is in reality
a denial of God or atheism. Pantheism comes about as a reaction to Deism, which contrariwise goes too far in separat-

ing God and the world. Deism admits the creation of the world by God but denies that He now sustains it. In short, it accepts His existence and at the same time denies His Providence and likewise the truth of Revelation and Christianity. Pantheism is a foggy, and sometimes artificially stimulated, sentiment of identification with the divine; it is a misguided yearning for salvation, which refuses to accept union with God humbly as His gift, but foolishly — and in last analysis with blasphemous pride — claims it as its right and due.

B. ST. PAUL'S HYMN OF PRAISE

"Blessed be the God and Father of our Lord Jesus Christ, who has blessed us with every spiritual blessing on high in Christ. Even as he chose us in him before the foundation of the world, that we should be holy and without blemish in his sight in love. He predestined us to be adopted through Jesus Christ as his sons, according to the purpose of his will, unto the praise of the glory of his grace, with which he has favored us in his beloved son.

"In him we have redemption through his blood, the remission of sins, according to the riches of his grace. This grace has abounded beyond measure in us in all wisdom and prudence, so that he may make known to us the mystery of His will according to his good pleasure. And this his good pleasure he purposed in him to be dispensed in the fullness of the times: to re-establish all things, in Christ, both those in the heavens and those on the earth.

"In him, I say, in whom we also have been called by a special choice, having been predestined in the purpose of him who works all things according to the counsel of his will, to contribute to the praise of his glory — we who before hoped in Christ. And in him you too, when you had heard the word of truth, the good news of your salvation, and believed in it, were sealed with the Holy Spirit of the promise, who is the pledge of our inheritance, for a redemption of possession, for the praise of his glory" (Eph. 1:3—14).

C. DOGMA AND THE ECCLESIASTICAL YEAR

The sacred liturgy is celebrated as a continuous memorial and re-presentation of the mystery of the Redemption. Accordingly it vitalizes the full content of dogmatic truths, which become real and stream into the activities of our daily life. The connection between life and dogma is very close indeed.

The several cycles of the ecclesiastical year are the means used to present this re-enactment of the mysteries of our Redemption in a manner spirited and progressive. Every Holy Mass is the complete re-enactment of Christ's redemptive work. The Church, on Her part, permits us to draw piecemeal upon the sacred mystery of Christ's life, and to translate it into our own. When, during the weeks of Advent, she has awakened in us a consciousness of our need of redemption, she begins thereafter to unfold the sacred mystery of Christ's life and presents the person of Christ and His blessed Mother as the center of the Christmas cycle. The Feast of Easter once again prompts us to renew our life in the Saviour's redemptive work: His death and resurrection. The Easter cycle, and we emphasize this, includes the Feast of Pentecost. The long series of Sundays after Pentecost are like a prolonged meditation on the working out of the fruits of the Redemption operating in us through the Holy Ghost.

Naturally we do not expect to find a strictly systematic

treatise of Christ's life in the ecclesiastical year. The liturgy represents life, and life is scarcely a rigid system. Consider, for instance, the prominent place given Adam and original sin during the pre-lenten season rather than during Advent. Again, the diligent observer will remark how the passage and progress of the ecclesiastical year is closely akin to and keeps pace with the Christian growth expressed in Ephesians 1:3–14 (cf. Appendix II B). Indeed, that excerpt from St. Paul's Epistle gives one the impression of a liturgical hymn.

The life of the liturgy will crystallize in the life of the Christian who lives with the Church. In addition, such a one will readily assimilate the spiritual content of the ecclesiastical year. Furthermore, only he who obtains this all-embracing view into the nature of Christianity will be able "to live the liturgy" fruitfully and intelligently and so translate it into his own life. That is why St. Paul insists on the value of knowledge for the spiritual life (Eph. 1:17). Thus dogmatic teaching and active participation in the liturgy complement and enrich each other. Consequently together they provide the true Christian life.

D. REMARKS ON THE HISTORY OF DOGMA

Dogma is the form, stamped by the infallible teaching office of the Church acting under the abiding presence of the Holy Ghost, in which the truths of faith find their expression. Hence dogma is essentially constant and unalterable. It neither can nor does establish a new truth. Likewise, what has once been true cannot pass away.

Dogma, however, undergoes change inasmuch as men and the Church undergo change; these can and must grow and develop in the understanding of Revelation. Thus a dogma can, in the course of time, become more fully apprehended and appreciated. Furthermore, a new and better form of presentation, one which more adequately renders the "sense" of Revelation, can be discovered. In this clearer rendering of the sense of Revelation lies the development of dogma.

Even in the earliest times, the Church Fathers sought to elucidate dogmatic development by the use of comparisons drawn from the growth of living substances.

"Progress requires that the subject become enlarged, developed, in itself; alteration, that part of the one be changed into something else. The intelligence, therefore, the knowledge, the wisdom, of the individual as well as of the whole Church, ought, according to the advance of age and time, to increase, and make much and vigorous progress — but yet only in its own kind, i.e., in the same doctrine, in the same sense, and in the same meaning.

"The growth of religion in souls must be analogous to the growth of the body, which, though in the course of years it develops and attains full stature, yet remains fundamentally the same. There is a great difference between the flower of youth and the maturity of age; yet they who were once young are still the same now that they have become old. Though the stature and outward form of the individual are changed, yet his nature is one and the same, his person is one and the same." (Vincent of Lerins, *A Commonitory,* 23.)

Just as the acorn one day becomes an oak, so, too, with time, has the early Church become in Her dogmatic teaching the Church of our times. Through the gradual unfolding of dogma, as explained above, it becomes evident that Christianity is a real life; that dogma is not a "dead-letter" teaching but a living one. This development of dogma is carried out by the teaching function of the Church. It is conducted under the power of the Holy Spirit, the Spirit of truth of whom Christ said "He will teach you all the truth" (John 16:13).

Human minds and strength, however, serve to stimulate and hasten the development of dogma under the control of Divine Providence. The occasion is usually given by some heretical attack on the truth. The even tenor of development thereby ensues.

There is, let us say, a revealed truth which has always been taken for granted by the Church, perhaps implicitly so, but which is now called into doubt. (It is self-evident that the Church owns these truths much as a man owns health when he is well.) Then follow prolonged discussion and painstaking deep thought on the matter. Theological skill is engaged to dissipate the heresy and to invalidate its difficulties and objections. Sometimes in the course of this work theological science itself falls into temporary error. Finally, the teaching office of the Church establishes, once and for all, what is the truth about revelation and what is error in regard to it (Schmaus). Furthermore, disputed questions between theologians can contribute to the development of doctrine. So can, finally, the calm contemplation of truth on the part of a great soul eminent for his love of truth.

The scientific presentation of dogmatic development is called the history of dogma. Its office is to give an exposition of dogma: as to how, throughout diverse times, dogma has unfolded itself at different periods in the history of the Church. Hence it follows that the history of dogma is part of the history of the Church, and contributes its share to the "building up of the body of Christ . . . to perfect manhood, the mature measure of the fullness of Christ" (Eph. 4:13).

STUDY OUTLINE

INTRODUCTION

1. Religion
   Man's need of God
   Purpose of religion in the universe
   Communal need of religion
2. Knowledge of God
   By faith — Sources $\begin{cases} \text{Scripture} \\ \text{Tradition} \end{cases}$

   By revelation — Sources $\begin{cases} \text{Teaching of Church through Pope, etc.} \\ \text{Infallibility of Church in these matters} \\ \text{Councils} \end{cases}$

PART I

GOD AND HIS ETERNAL PLAN OF CREATION

1. God
   a) Triune God
      Revelation
      Christ's words *in re*
      Their relationship in their identity considered as a mystery
      Knowable in analogies
      Doctrine set forth by Council of Florence
      Dogma considered in everyday life

b) **God the Father**
  (1) Knowable
    By acquiescence in His perfection
    By comparison with created beings
    By elimination of limits in creatures
    We cannot know God thoroughly
  (2) Nature of (cf. Garrigou-Lagrange) (cited in reference books)
    He is a being
    He is capable of thought
    He can will
    His existence is in Himself
    His existence is without limitation (He is)
  (3) Attributes of (cf. Garrigou-Lagrange)

    (*a*) Being
        He is eternal and unchanging
        He is without time
        He is immense
        He is omnipresent

    (*b*) Intellect
        He is from all time
        His knowledge is "now"
        He is all wise "Being First Cause"

    (*c*) Will
        He is almighty — Power of His will
        He is goodness — He cannot will evil — Source of goodness — presents good to our intellect — we accept or refuse — free will
        He is just
        He is merciful — Knows all things — Does not immediately punish

    (*d*) Summary
        Perfection of Divine Will
        Perfection of Divine Knowledge:
          (1) He is all truth — cannot err, since His knowledge is one with His holiness
          (2) He is all faithful — He will keep His promises

2. **Creation**
  a) Material World
    (1) The Word of the Son of God
    (2) We exist through Him — we are products of His essence

(3) We exist for a knowable reason
(4) We depend on God — our existence comes from Him, therefore we love Him since He designs our life, i.e., we must love our end
(5) He permits physical and moral evil (suffering and trials) for a purpose. Since He is the source, His will can attain only the good

b) Spiritual World
(1) The Mediator
(2) He created the Spirit World (angels)
(3) He created angels for government of world; they possess will, intellect
(4) Angels and men created from goodness of God, since he doesn't need either
(5) Favorite is man — Since He created Him to His image and likeness. Man was endowed with spiritual faculties for knowing God
(6) Loss of knowledge of God is through sin
(7) Spirit of God imprinted through Holy Spirit (sanctifying grace)

PART II

EXECUTION OF THE PLAN OF REDEMPTION

1. Redemption
a) Necessity of
(1) Man created perfect (i.e., in beginning of time) and therefore possessed all gifts — immortality, inferior parts of nature subject to reason
(2) Lost perfect and complete happiness in Adam's sin of pride, or refusal to admit dependence on God
(3) Man lost immortality, sanctifying grace, knowing intellect, etc.
(4) Man inherited pain, suffering, a tendency to evil — original sin (but with promise of a Redeemer)
(5) Man lost and inherited this through Adam, the first man. Adam transmitted this state of sin to all creatures
(6) Sin demands punishment since offense is against the

almighty God; divine satisfaction since sin is affront to divinity; therefore Son of God became Man

2. The Redeemer
   a) Christ
      (1) True God as proven by occasions in His life on earth, miracles, etc.
      (2) True man for He had human emotions, trials, etc.
      (3) By Incarnation Son of God became Mediator between God and man; became the God-Man, human and divine but one person
   b) Christ's Mother
      (1) Virgin — perpetual, i.e., before and after birth of Christ Christ's last words
      (2) Immaculate Conception — in view of merits of Christ she was preserved free from original sin
      (3) Body assumed into heaven
      (4) Coadjutor in the Redemption of man
3. The redemptive act
   a) Adam sinned by disobedience
   b) Christ had to atone by perfect act of obedience obedience — life of sacrifice here on earth and death on the cross
4. The results
   a) By Redemptive Act
      (1) Heaven and earth are reconciled
      (2) We { are delivered from power of devil
              participate in Christ expiation (He died for all men)
              are saved depending on our use of our free will
5. Redeemer must be risen, i.e., arise from the dead and take possession of this glorified life in heaven
6. Merits of redemption
   a) Baptism (union) erases original sin, i.e., we partake of Him (also other sacraments)
   b) Love — gaining the Holy Spirit who is the expression of love in the Trinity
   c) Gain Holy Spirit in Christ, i.e., in His humanity — operation of Holy Spirit within us refers to the spiritualized Christ

Part III

SANCTIFICATION

1. Holy Spirit
   a) In man — through incorporation in Christ (Sonship of God)
   b) Fashions and deifies man since He deifies and glorifies the humanity of Christ
   c) Works within us (incorporated in Christ — state of sanctifying grace)
   d) Man receiving enlightenment on a particular occasion — state of actual grace
2. Grace
   a) Necessary for salvation — but exerts no compulsion on part of man — Man must cooperate but he may resist (free will)
   b) Sanctifying grace is likeness to God, the high life of soul
   c) Actual grace is momentary activity of God in soul for every work conducive to spiritual life.
3. Church teaches (Grace)
   a) God gives sufficient grace to all men that they may fully believe. If man cooperates with grace he has will to do good. The more good we do the more we increase in sanctifying grace and merit life everlasting
   b) Fullness of the Holy Spirit when creature thinks, wills, and works toward God
   c) Grace brings the theological virtues of faith, hope, and charity; four cardinal virtues of prudence, justice, fortitude, and temperance; and seven gifts of the Holy Spirit, spirit of wisdom, understanding, knowledge, counsel, fortitude, piety, and fear of the Lord
      These lead men to the divine inspirations required to attain eternal happiness
4. Church teaches
   a) By loss of grace, through one mortal sin, we lose all that it gives and brings
   b) We lose by thought, word, and deed
   c) Mortal sin, death of soul, destroys Sonship of God

   Conditions } grave matter
              sufficient reflection, full consent of will

d) Venial sin — any transgression of Law of God lacking any one of the above three conditions for grievous sin

PART IV

THE CHURCH — "BODY OF CHRIST"

1. Nature
   a) Exists in social character of man — Created by God, man fell into sin, drew race with him

   b) Christ
       Church } are one — Christ is head { exists independently of His Church; existed before His Church; contains the fullness of grace which God bestows on man (Eph. 4:15–16; Col. 1:17–20; 2:9–10; 3:15; and I Cor. 12:4–27)

   c) Holy Spirit is soul of this body (the Church) — He lives in Christ, is life principle, font of graces to members
2. Members
   a) Equality { united with Christ according to each one's worth determined by manner of fulfilling place in the divine plan
   b) Nations called to the Church (I Cor. 13)
3. Conclusion
   a) Church is continuation of Christ in time
   b) A society { Church Triumphant
                   Church Militant
                   Church Suffering
   c) Church has four marks: one — is Christ on earth; holy — is Christ Himself; catholic — is universal; apostolic — is founded on the apostles — no interruption in succession
   d) Church is necessary
       (1) Through it alone can we be saved
       (2) But persons in good faith can be sincere in eyes of God;

therefore, will is considered here more than the deed.
Sufficient graces therefore will be given for salvation.
e) Church is the Living Christ
Carries on His mission by liturgy or worship, i.e., done in
His name and at His command
(1) Sacrifice of Mass
(2) Unites sufferings to Christ's sufferings; teaching;
governing

Part V

THE SACRAMENTS

1. What they are:
   a) Means of grace is outward sign — is instituted by Christ,
   by which His grace is conferred on us
   b) Seven in number:
   (1) Baptism; (2) Holy Eucharist; (3) Holy Orders; (4)
   Confirmation; (5) Penance; (6) Matrimony; (7)
   Extreme Unction
   c) Outward sign

   matter $\begin{cases} \text{rites} \\ \text{ceremonies} \\ \text{material used} \end{cases}$ $\begin{cases} \text{form — words that determine application} \\ \text{of rites, ceremonies, and materials used} \end{cases}$

   d) All are adapted to man (spiritual-corporeal). Sacrament is a
   symbol containing what it expresses
   e) They are
   (1) Continuation of Christ's activity (incarnation)
   (2) Ministered by Christ (the author) human instrument is
   priest
   (3) Effective, i.e., not dependent on disposition of human
   instrument
   (4) Divine in character since they draw out man from root
   of his being and improve his will to do good
   (5) To be received with intention to receive them and with
   desire of receiving grace
   f) Unchangeable in their essence. Entrusted to care of the

   Church who must legislate for $\begin{cases} \text{worthy reception} \\ \text{worthy administration} \end{cases}$

2. What they do:

a) Sacraments *confer grace* on us since they bring us in contact with God and effect infusion of sanctifying grace

b) Known as {
Sacrament of the Dead — Infuses sanctifying
grace
Sacrament of the Living — Increases it (grace)

c) They
(1) Have sacramental grace or a claim to actual grace necessary for life corresponding to the nature of the
sacrament received
(2) Impress indelible marks (character) on soul, i.e.:
(*a*) Baptism — a general priesthood
(*b*) Confirmation — develops this priestly character
(*c*) Holy Orders — official priesthood

d) Their Reception
(1) Spiritual — i.e., having will and intellect
(2) Corporeal — manifested externally

e) Sacramentals — Resemble sacraments — are instituted by
Church
(1) Blessed objects — holy water, etc.
(2) Their use holy — effects are not infallible

3. The seven sacraments
a) Baptism
(1) Nature
(*a*) First and most important — destroys original sin
(Mark 16:15–16; John 3:5)
(*b*) Water is outward sign — also words used in form
(*c*) Water need not be baptismal water; if necessary
natural water may be used
(*d*) Instituted by Christ (Matt. 28:18, 20)
(*e*) Is rebirth from water — Incorporation in Christ
(Rom. 6:3–8; Gal. 2:19–20)
(2) Effects
(*a*) Destroys original sin — unites us with Christ
(*b*) Indelibly impresses our souls with character of
Christ
(*c*) Qualifies one to receive the other sacraments (I
Pet. 2:5)

b) Confirmation
(1) Nature
(*a*) Strengthens that which baptism implants

(*b*) Sacrament of Holy Spirit
(*c*) Develops baptismal character in order to cooperate in common good of Church
(*d*) Bestows gift of Holy Spirit (Acts 8:14, 17; 19:6)
(*e*) Administered (ordinarily) by a bishop

(2) Effects
    (*a*) Increases sanctifying grace
    (*b*) Impresses indelible character
    (*c*) Confers Holy Spirit
    (*d*) Implants fearlessness
    (*e*) Increases apostolic zeal

c) Holy Eucharist — A sacrament
(1) Nature
    (*a*) Sacramental Presence of Christ (John 6:1–15, 16–21, 22–71). Christ's words at Last Supper
    (*b*) Manner of Presence (one substance to another)
      i) Transubstantial
      ii) Words of Consecration at Holy Mass
    (*c*) Symbol of Shedding of Blood — Sacraments are God given and contain the reality they symbolize
    (*d*) Holy Mass not a repetition but a renewal — Christ's words "Do this in commemoration of Me" (Heb. 9:25; 10:11)
    (*e*) Christ is Priest and Victim (human priest — instrument)
    (*f*) Through Mass we participate in the redemptive sacrifice of Christ
    (*g*) Intimate participation in Christ's Sacrifice by Holy Communion, since we partake of Body and Blood of Christ

(2) Effects
    (*a*) Increases sanctifying grace
    (*b*) Weakens evil tendencies
    (*c*) Gives power for good
    (*d*) Gives joy
    (*e*) Cleanses us of venial sins
    (*f*) Guards against mortal sin
    (*g*) Gives life everlasting
    (*h*) Glorious resurrection of the body (John 6:54)
    (*i*) Sacrament of Living — being a food — is union with

God and with men — administered under form of bread (practical)

d) Penance (A sacrament)
  (1) Nature
    (a) Is forgiveness of all sins committed after baptism
    (b) Instituted by Christ on His Resurrection (John 20:22)
    (c) Priest is judge $\left\{\begin{array}{l}\text{must know the sins, etc.}\\ \text{sinner must be sincere}\\ \text{must tell the sins — kind and number}\end{array}\right.$
    (d) Possesses external signs $\left\{\begin{array}{l}\text{1. confession}\\ \text{2. expressed contrition}\\ \text{3. words of priest — form}\end{array}\right.$
    (e) Church requires by the fifth commandment that the faithful confess at least once a year
  (2) Requisites
    (a) Examination of conscience
    (b) Contrition (most important) matter of the will
      i) *Perfect* — from soul — out of love of God eradicates sin directly. But there is an obligation to confess a mortal sin — for perfect contrition will include a resolve to confess
      ii) *Imperfect* — from fear
    (c) Firm purpose of amendment
    (d) Confession — should be (1) Absolute — the sin and circumstances (obligation to confess mortal sin; no obligation to confess venial sin). (2) Sincere — Direct accusation of self in all particulars. (3) Clear — without attempt to hide or gloss over facts
    (e) Satisfaction — imposed by priest in penance. Penitent must at least will reparation
  (3) Effects
    (a) Confession increases sanctifying grace
    (b) Remits sin
    (c) Remits eternal and at least part of temporal punishment due to sin
    (d) Conveys actual grace
  (4) Indulgences

(*a*) Nature
  i) Is remission of temporal punishment due to sins already forgiven
  ii) Is not a remission of sin
  iii) Church by power of remission or retaining can substitute penances
  iv) State of sanctifying grace is necessary for gaining an indulgence

(*b*) Kinds
  i) Plenary — remission of *all* temporal punishment due to sin. *In order to be gained,* person must: confess; receive Holy Communion; visit church; pray for interest of Holy Father
  ii) Partial — remission of part of temporal punishment due to sin

e) Holy Orders
 (1) Nature
   (*a*) Is conferring of priestly powers and grace to lead a priestly life
   (*b*) Is conferred by a bishop — Imposition of Hands
   (*c*) Is divided into

   Minor Orders { Ostiary — Porter
   Lector — Reader
   Exorcist
   Acolyte }

   Major Orders { Subdiaconate
   Diaconate
   Priesthood }

 (2) Effects
   (*a*) Power of priesthood (to consecrate and bless, administer the sacraments, forgive sin)
   (*b*) Instituted by Christ at Last Supper when He conferred these powers, it imprints on soul priesthood of Christ. Priest is representative of Christ

f) Matrimony
 (1) Nature
   (*a*) Instituted by God in Paradise (Gen. 2:22)
   (*b*) Its essence is in unity of { one man
   one woman } { indissoluble (Matt. 19:3–9; Luke 16: 18) }

(c) Symbolizes union of Christ and Church
(d) Confers grace it symbolizes — because it is a sacrament and union of man and woman must be: faithful; permanent; holy
(e) Impediments — Church legislates since it is a sacrament (divine authority)
    i) diriment — Blood relationship
    ii) hindering — Mixed marriage
(2) Purpose
    (a) Mutual perfection of man and wife
    (b) Procreation of human race
    (c) Regulation of sex impulses
g) Extreme Unction
  (1) Nature
    (a) By which a sick (seriously) person receives grace of God for salvation of soul, and often for welfare and strength of body
    (b) By priest to only the seriously ill and only once in same illness
    (c) By anointing of eyes, ears, nose, mouth, hands, feet with oil (senses)
    (d) By use of form (words) (St. James 5:14)
  (2) Effects
    (a) Increases grace
    (b) Destroys sin and punishment or part of it
    (c) Relieves temptation
    (d) Gives patience and confidence

PART VI

THE CONSUMMATION

1. Death — Judgment (Heb. 9:27; Rom. 5:12)
  a) Death brings
        Earthly life to an end
        Start of immortal life
  b) Particular judgment — St. Augustine
2. Eternal Death
  a) To those in state of mortal sin
  b) Doctrine (Matt. 25:41; Mark 9:44)

    c) Damned person hates God since He is opposed to Him
    Damned person realizes loss of heaven and happiness
    Damned person realizes pain of separation
    Damned person realizes loss of Beatific Vision
    Damned person realizes positive pain in body according
       to degree of guilt
    Damned person realizes He has chosen hell (free will)
    d) Existence of hell postulated from God's justice
3. Eternal Life
    a) To one dying in God's grace
    b) Merited by deeds in life
    c) Purgatory
        (1) Person evidently not pure enough to enter immediately
            into eternal happiness
        (2) Undergone willingly — from knowledge of distance be-
            tween God and themselves (II Mach. 12:14)
        (3) Greatest suffering is exclusion from sight of God, but,
            since there is knowledge of eternal salvation, they
            enjoy benefit therefrom
        (4) Is place therefore of love and surrender to God's holy
            will
        (5) Upon completion of purgation period soul enters into
            bliss of heaven
    d) Sainthood — Church
        { By investigation of life of an indi-
           vidual (practice of virtue to an
           heroic degree)
           Proclaims infallibly that such a
           person attaining bliss of heaven
           is worthy of veneration as a saint
    e) Eternal Happiness is
        (1) Sight of God — immersion in Him
        (2) Without bodily limitation (regaining faculties lost by
            sin of Adam) (Cor. 13:12; Cer. 2:9; Phil. 3:20)
        (3) Admits different degrees of happiness, i.e., who loves
            God more will receive more, yet all enjoy complete
            satisfaction of their lot
4. General Judgment — Signs
    a) Catastrophe (Matt. 24:6–8)
    b) Anti-Christ (II Thess. 2:1–7; Matt. 24:24; II Thess. 2:9–11)
    c) Phenomena of the heavens
    d) Appearance of Christ (Matt. 24:30; 24:27; 24:31; John

5:28, 29; Matt. 16:27; 25:3–11; Luke 21:28; II Thess. 2:8; II Pet. 3:7–12)

e) At End of Time (Col. 1:16; Matt. 3; Luke 3:17; Matt. 12:30; John 5:22–23; Ps. 109–111; Ps. 8:8; I Cor. 15: 24–28)

APPENDIX IV

REFERENCE BOOKS

The following bibliography has been selected by James A. Quinn, O.P., so as to further interest in the study of the sacred sciences.

SACRED SCRIPTURE

Lagrange, J. M., O.P., *The Gospel of Jesus Christ* (Burns, Oates and Washbourne, London).

Goodier, Alban, S.J., *The Public Life of Christ* (P. J. Kenedy & Sons, New York).

——— *Dogma and Church Fathers.*

Otten, Bernard J., S.J., *Manual of the History of Dogma* (Herder, St. Louis).

Pohle, J., and Preuss, A., *Series of Dogmatic Textbooks* (Herder, St. Louis).

Tixeront, J., *A Handbook of Patrology* (Herder, St. Louis).

——— *History of Dogma,* 3 vols. (Herder, St. Louis).

Cayré, F., *Manual of Patrology,* 2 vols. (Desclée & Co., Tournai).

——— *The Ante-Nicene Fathers* (Scribner & Sons, New York).

——— *The Post-Nicene Fathers* (Scribner & Sons, New York).

POPULAR WORKS

Jarrett, B., O.P., *The Abiding Presence of the Holy Ghost* (Burns, Oates & Washbourne, London).

Prat, Fernand, S.J., *Theology of St. Paul,* 2 vols. (Burns, Oates & Washbourne, London).

Benson, Robert Hugh, *Christ in the Church* (Sheed & Ward, New York).

Dawson, Christopher, *Medieval Religion* (Sheed & Ward, New York).

Sertillanges, A., O.P., *The Church* (Burns, Oates & Washbourne, London).

Puniet, Jean de, *The Mass — Its Origin and History* (Longmans, Green, New York).

Garrigou-Lagrange, Reginald, O.P., *God: His Essence and Existence,* 2 vols. (Herder, St. Louis).

Farrell, Walter, O.P., *Companion to the Summa,* 2 vols. (Sheed & Ward, New York).

Walshe, T. J., *Principles of Catholic Apologetics* (Herder, St. Louis).

Pius XI, *Caritate Christi Compulsi* (America Press, New York).

Dawson, Christopher, *The Making of Europe* (Sheed & Ward, New York).

Michel, Virgil, O.S.B., *Our Life in Christ* (Liturgical Press, Collegeville, Minn.).

Adam, Karl, *Christ Our Brother* (The Macmillan Co., New York).

——— *The Son of God* (Sheed & Ward, New York).

Marmion, Columba, O.S.B., *Christ The Life of the Soul* (Herder, St. Louis).

Sheed, F. J., *A Map of Life* (Sheed & Ward, New York).

Vonier, Anscar, O.S.B., *The Key to the Doctrine of the Eucharist* (Burns, Oates & Washbourne, London).

"The Truth of Christianity" Series (Benziger Brothers, New York) for study clubs.

LITURGY

Guardini, Romano, *The Church and The Catholic, The Spirit of the Liturgy* (Sheed & Ward, New York).

Michel, Virgil, O.S.B. (in collaboration with other authors), *The Christ-Life Series* (Liturgical Press, Collegeville, Minn.).

Loeher, Bernard C., *Following Christ Through the Mass* (Bruce, Milwaukee).

Cabrol, Abbot, O.S.B., *Liturgical Prayer* (Burns, Oates & Washbourne, London).

Schuster, Ildefons, O.S.B., *The Sacramentary,* 5 vols. (Burns, Oates & Washbourne, London).

The Day Hours (Liturgical Press, Collegeville, Minn.).

The Roman Breviary and Roman Missal (Liturgical Press, Collegeville, Minn.).

Popular Liturgical Library (Liturgical Press, Collegeville, Minn.).

Orate Fratres, A Monthly Liturgical Review (Liturgical Press, Collegeville, Minn.).

INDEX